Cambridge Elements

Elements in the Gothic
edited by
Dale Townshend
Manchester Metropolitan University
Angela Wright
University of Sheffield

GOTHIC DEMENTIA

Troubled Minds in Gothic Timelines

Laura R. Kremmel
Niagara University

Shaftesbury Road, Cambridge CB2 8EA, United Kingdom

One Liberty Plaza, 20th Floor, New York, NY 10006, USA

477 Williamstown Road, Port Melbourne, VIC 3207, Australia

314–321, 3rd Floor, Plot 3, Splendor Forum, Jasola District Centre, New Delhi – 110025, India

Cambridge University Press is part of Cambridge University Press & Assessment, a department of the University of Cambridge.

We share the University's mission to contribute to society through the pursuit of education, learning and research at the highest international levels of excellence.

www.cambridge.org
Information on this title: www.cambridge.org/9781009576970

DOI: 10.1017/9781009576994

© Laura R. Kremmel 2026

This publication is in copyright. Subject to statutory exception and to the provisions of relevant collective licensing agreements, no reproduction of any part may take place without the written permission of Cambridge University Press & Assessment.

When citing this work, please include a reference to the DOI 10.1017/9781009576994

First published 2026

A catalogue record for this publication is available from the British Library

A Cataloging-in-Publication data record for this Element is available from the Library of Congress

ISBN 978-1-009-57697-0 Hardback
ISBN 978-1-009-57696-3 Paperback
ISSN 2634-8721 (online)
ISSN 2634-8713 (print)

Cambridge University Press & Assessment has no responsibility for the persistence or accuracy of URLs for external or third-party internet websites referred to in this publication and does not guarantee that any content on such websites is, or will remain, accurate or appropriate.

For EU product safety concerns, contact us at Calle de José Abascal, 56, 1°, 28003 Madrid, Spain, or email eugpsr@cambridge.org

Gothic Dementia

Troubled Minds in Gothic Timelines

Elements in the Gothic

DOI: 10.1017/9781009576994
First published online: March 2026

Laura R. Kremmel
Niagara University
Author for correspondence: Laura R. Kremmel, LauraRKremmel@gmail.com

Abstract: *Gothic Dementia: Troubled Minds in Gothic Timelines* introduces Gothic studies as a valuable lens through which to critically consider how we think about dementia. It argues that the Gothic's foundational narrative techniques can model approaches to similar dementia symptoms, such as chronological confusion, fragmentation, cyclical storytelling, repetition, unreliable narrators, unstable identities, uncanny behaviours, and Otherness. If we can navigate these challenging narrative elements in literature, can we navigate similar challenging dementia signs using interpretive strategies? Gothic Dementia considers this question in two ways: (1) through Gothic literary elements that correlate to characteristics of dementia and (2) through contentious horror film depictions of characters with dementia and their caregivers. Reading Gothic works and horror films within the context of dementia studies—and vice versa—can contribute valuable insights into a feared disease that threatens the core of who we imagine ourselves and others to be.

Keywords: Gothic, dementia, British Literature, medicine, horror film

© Laura R. Kremmel 2026

ISBNs: 9781009576970 (HB), 9781009576963 (PB), 9781009576994 (OC)
ISSNs: 2634-8721 (online), 2634-8713 (print)

Contents

1 Introduction: Gothic Rhetorics of Cognitive Dis-ease   1

2 Cycles of Fear: Fragmentation and Temporal Confusion   14

3 Ageing Supernaturally: Dementia in Immortality   28

4 Lost Selves: The Demon in Dementia   41

5 Uncanny Connections: Caregivers and Caretakers   55

  Bibliography   68

1 Introduction: Gothic Rhetorics of Cognitive Dis-ease

The Gothic is obsessed with time, even more than with atmosphere and environment: architectural ruins decayed by history, underground crypts containing centuries of ancestry, haunted characters who refuse to modernise. The return of the repressed is defined by past events intruding into the present. Cycles of abuse advance and retreat in repetitive bubbles of temporal flux. Chris Baldick's frequently referenced definition of the Gothic includes 'a fearful sense of inheritance in time' combined with a 'claustrophobic sense of enclosure in space, these two dimensions reinforcing one another to produce an impression of sickening descent into disintegration'.[1] Time may be shared, passed on, obtained, or lost. It may also entrap, devour, erase, or withhold. In Gothic narratives, time is not a progressive march forward towards hope; it is an inescapable residual dread that, despite evidence of age and decay, we have been here before and will be again. This includes the impact of time on human bodies and minds. Confused timelines, lost memories, and blurred distinctions between past and present are all sources of dis-ease that the Gothic regularly applies. They are also typical descriptions of dementia.

This distinctive relationship with time, combined with a tendency to push minds and bodies beyond their limits and to side with abnormal and monstrous Others, makes the Gothic well placed to challenge preconceived notions of human health and medicine. In this Element, I explore the benefits of considering dementia through the lens of Gothic approaches to time, narrative, and identity. Dementia, among other stigmatised illnesses like cancer and addiction, tends to be spoken of in hushed tones, behind closed doors, as people with the disease may be silenced and shut away. Discomfort with dementia is so powerful that its very suggestion prompts hearers to reassess their own lifestyles and pour money into preventative treatments that often bear little evidence of success. Once a diagnosis is suspected, it may initiate social avoidance, complicate familial relationships, and interfere with human rights. In daily parlance, dementia is casually considered by some to be worse than a death sentence, an illness from which no one recovers and that curses a home with financial and emotional strain. In short, amongst the general public, dementia is currently considered to be a horror. As such, I suggest potential approaches to read and navigate these perceptions of dread, informed by Gothic studies, dementia studies, disability studies, and age studies. This Element, then, considers interactions between the Gothic and dementia in two ways: (1) through Gothic conventions that correlate to symptoms of dementia and thus offer unique

---

[1] Chris Baldick, 'Introduction', in Chris Baldick (ed.), *The Oxford Book of Gothic Tales* (Oxford: Oxford University Press, 2009), pp. xi–xxiii (p. xix).

insights by putting them in the context of generic literary interpretation independent of deficit-based judgements and (2) through the contentious and deliberate horror film depictions of dementia that are problematic but also critically valuable for their exposure of the challenges associated with dementia care and its realignment of power dynamics. From both angles, I argue that reading Gothic works within the context of dementia and vice versa can contribute valuable insights to the ongoing debates within the field of dementia studies. This Element offers ways of reframing dementia – how symptoms are interpreted, how it is talked about, how those with dementia are treated, and how care is provided – through the context of Gothic literature and film.

1.1 Dementia Histories and Dementia Studies

Despite the attention it has gained in the twenty-first century, dementia is not just a modern term. The earliest usage listed by the *OED* dates back to the sixteenth century (1598) to describe a madness characterised by impaired judgement or intellect, specifying that it was only later related to memory. Dementia was believed to be temporary and curable in these early centuries. The term is included in eighteenth-century medical dictionaries to indicate simply 'madness or a delirium'[2] and was not yet considered to be age-related as cognitive decline had long been deemed an expected and 'natural' part of senescence. Jesse Ballenger notes that, despite shifting definitions of this term, 'everything we know about the natural history of age-associated progressive dementia suggests that it has always been part of human experience, yet only in the modern era has it been regarded as a disease', though even today its precise relationship to age is debated.[3]

Early French psychiatrist Jean Etienne Dominique Esquirol uses 'dementia' to indicate an age-related psychological disorder, but even his descriptions in *Mental Maladies: A Treatise on Insanity* (1838) include age as related rather than required. Instead, he focuses on symptoms associated with coherent narrative processing: 'weakening of the sensibility, understanding and will.... Man in a state of dementia, has lost the faculty of perceiving objects correctly, of seizing upon their relations, comparing them, and producing a distinct remembrance of them'. When conversing with others, their speech may be illogical and they 'repeat words and entire sentences, without attaching to them any precise

---

[2] John Quincy, *Lexicon Physico-Medicum; Or, a New Medicinal Dictionary Explaining the Difficult Terms Used in the Several Branches of the Profession and in Such Parts of Natural Philosophy*, 11th ed (London: Longman, 1794), p. 265.

[3] Jesse Ballenger, 'Dementia: Confusion at the Borderlands of Aging and Madness', in Greg Eghigian (ed.), *The Routledge History of Madness and Mental Health* (London: Routledge, 2017), pp. 297–311 (p. 297).

signification' as they struggle to remember even recent occurrences.[4] Some of Esquirol's description even sounds like literary analysis, encouraging more aggressive narrative navigation than is typical because 'we clearly perceive breaks, which it would be necessary to fill up, in order to give to their discourses the arrangement, filiation and perfection, which belongs to a connected and complete process of reasoning', suggesting that reading practices rather than the 'text' itself may require adjustment. Even more Gothic, Esquirol describes people with dementia as ghostly imitations of themselves, uninterested in anything or anyone whose importance previously defined their identities, like spouses and children.[5] Only when he breaks down the scale of his study into trends and statistics does Esquirol get into the involvement of age as one of dementia's major causes, much more than 'menstrual disorders', 'falls upon the head', 'abuses of wine', 'masturbation' and 'moral causes' like 'frights'. He notes that most cases are seen in patients between forty and eighty, with younger cases restricted to the upper class.[6] Thus, though age is a major source of dementia, he in no way assumes that people will commonly get dementia as they age. Dementia's association with age was formalised in the nineteenth century as 'senile dementia', though this is now considered to be a derogatory term. Philippe Pinel, who worked closely with Esquirol, also used it to describe an emotional pathology occurring later in life.

Partially motivated by the promise of funding for discovering new diseases, early twentieth-century pathologists divided dementia into 'presenile' (under age sixty) and 'senile', which paved the way for Alois Alzheimer and August Deter to theorise today's most well-known iteration of dementia, Alzheimer's disease.[7] Furthermore, most scientists only partially accepted these distinctions, not fully convinced that there was enough difference between them to justify their distinct classifications.[8] As Fletcher writes, 'Somewhat ironically, as dementia has been reconfigured in relation to ageing, the earlier members of the category (those with young onset) have become increasingly estranged.'[9] The fluctuation of dementia's association with age and the nature of that

---

[4] Jean Étienne Dominique Esquirol, *Mental Maladies: A Treatise on Insanity*, trans. E. K. Hunt (Philadelphia: Lea and Blanchard, 1845), pp. 417–418.

[5] Esquirol, *Mental Maladies*, p. 418. [6] Esquirol, *Mental Maladies*, pp. 423–424.

[7] James Rupert Fletcher, 'Pathologisation, (Bio)medicalization and Biopolitics', in James Rupert Fletcher and Andrea Capstick (eds.), *A Critical History of Dementia Studies* (London: Routledge, 2024), pp. 13–26 (pp. 14–15); James Rupert Fletcher, *The Biopolitics of Dementia: A Neurocritical Perspective* (London: Routledge, 2024), pp. 21, 28–29.

[8] Fletcher, 'Pathologisation', pp. 14–15; Stephen Katz and Annette Leibing, '"Lost in Time Like Tears in Rain": Critical Perspectives on Personhood and Dementia', in Richard Ward and Linn J. Sandberg (eds.), *Critical Dementia Studies: An Introduction* (London: Routledge, 2023), pp. 57–71.

[9] Fletcher, 'Pathologisation', pp. 17–18.

association remind us that such definitions, including medical ones, are constructed and changeable, often for agendas beyond simply patient care. Dementia's association with age will be discussed more in Section 3.

Today, Alzheimer's disease indicates one of several more specific illnesses within the umbrella category of dementia. While Alzheimer's disease is common in people over sixty, official dementia organisations insist it is not part of 'normal' ageing. The CDC defines dementia as 'not a specific disease but rather a general term for the impaired ability to remember, think, or make decisions that interferes with doing everyday activities. Alzheimer's disease is the most common type of dementia'.[10] The National Institute of Health defines it as 'the loss of cognitive functioning – the ability to think, remember, or reason – to such an extent that it interferes with a person's daily life and activities', prefacing it with 'A diagnosis of dementia can be frightening for those affected by the syndrome, their family members, and caretakers'.[11] The National Health Service similarly defines dementia as 'a syndrome (a group of related symptoms) associated with an ongoing decline of brain functioning. There are many different causes of dementia, and many different types'.[12] Symptoms include 'problems' with memory, attention, communication, reasoning, and visual navigation, and the CDC further describes more specific behaviours like 'getting lost', 'using unusual words' and forgetting names and memories.[13] Not all symptoms appear at once. Difficulties retaining short-term memory and retrieving words are typical in the early stages, while a more substantive breakdown of communication and recall occurs in the late stages, along with changes in behaviour and mood and increasing difficulty performing basic self-care tasks.[14] Dementia is often reduced to this broad list of symptoms, but it is important to remember that it affects each person differently.

The range of this term, then, allows it to be widely applicable while still carrying a heavy amount of medical and cultural weight. In lieu of these different terms and histories, I intentionally use the term 'dementia' in this Element instead of 'Alzheimer's disease' because the former is a term whose

---

[10] CDC, 'About Dementia', *CDC: Alzheimer's Disease and Dementia*, 17 August 2024, www.cdc.gov/alzheimers-dementia/about/index.html [last accessed 20 June 2025].

[11] NIH, 'Dementias', *Health Information*, 20 October 2025, www.ninds.nih.gov/health-information/disorders/dementias [last accessed 16 November 2025].

[12] NHS, 'What Is Dementia', Health: A to Z, 20 July 2023, www.nhs.uk/conditions/dementia/about-dementia/what-is-dementia/ [last accessed 16 November 2025].

[13] CDC, 'Signs and Symptoms of Dementia', *CDC: Alzheimer's Disease and Dementia*, 14 August, 2024, www.cdc.gov/alzheimers-dementia/signs-symptoms/index.html [last accessed 20 June 2025].

[14] Joan Rahilly, 'Language Breakdown and the Construction of Meaning: Linguistic Frameworks for Readings of Dementia in Literature', in Tess Maginess (ed.), *Dementia and Literature: Interdisciplinary Perspectives* (London: Routledge, 2019), pp. 115–132 (p. 116).

broadness and inclusivity detracts from temptations to diagnose characters or texts. Age is, by necessity, a large part of my study but is not essential for texts to serve as readings of dementia experience. Neither are all narratives of ageing relevant for a study of dementia. Behaviours described as symptoms – with or without an official diagnosis under any of these shifting definitions – are plentiful throughout medicine, history, and literature and hint at a wide variety of creative methods to navigate them.

The academic field of Dementia studies grew out of concerns at the end of the twentieth century that people with dementia were experiencing dehumanisation and abuse within medical settings, a familiar concern to scholars in the health humanities and disability studies fields. Dawn Brooker describes the 'commonly held belief that those living with dementia did not experience physical pain'.[15] As recently as the 1980s and 1990s, a dementia diagnosis could incite neglect and abuse in formal care settings, and many would argue these experiences continue through today. Like most interdisciplinary fields, dementia studies encompasses different and often conflicting approaches under its umbrella, which makes its theories particularly dynamic while working towards the same goal: to support people with dementia and their networks of care in a culture that threatens their humanity and rights.

Dementia studies, then, largely defines itself in uncomfortable opposition to the medical model of disability as a dehumanising and deficit-focused approach, more concerned with diagnosis and 'fixing' what is 'wrong' than respecting quality of life.[16] However, as Hailee M. Yoshizaki-Gibbons points out, this is where disability studies and age studies clash, over the acceptance of medical intervention as necessary, even if a necessary evil.[17] In fact, Richard Ward and Linn J. Sandberg argue that neither disability studies nor gerontology has been historically willing to claim dementia because it may complicate the distance they have long worked to establish between themselves and the medical model as well as hopeful views of 'ageing gracefully'.[18] Dementia studies, then,

---

[15] Dawn Brooker, 'Person-Centred Dementia Care: The Legacy of Tom Kitwood', *International Journal of Percent-Centred Medicine* 12:2 (2022): 21–36 (p. 21).

[16] Andrea Capstick, 'The Century without a War: Kitwood's Concept of Malignant Social Psychology and the Need for Historicisation in Dementia Studies', in James Rupert Fletcher and Andrea Capstick (eds.), *A Critical History of Dementia Studies* (London: Routledge, 2024), pp. 27–37(p. 32).

[17] Hailee M. Yoshizaki-Gibbons, 'Ageism and Ableism on the Silvering Screen: Entanglements of Disability and Ageing in Films Centred on Dementia', in Sarah Falcus, Heike Hartung, and Raquel Medina (eds.), *The Bloomsbury Handbook to Ageing in Contemporary Literature and Film* (London: Bloomsbury, 2023), pp. 281–292 (p. 286).

[18] Linn J. Sandberg and Richard Ward, 'Introduction: Why Critical Dementia Studies and Why Now?' in Richard Ward and Linn J. Sandberg (eds.), *Critical Dementia Studies: An Introduction* (London: Routledge, 2023), pp. 1–12 (p. 2).

attempts to balance the ambivalent range of socio-political benefits and damages incurred by people with dementia within medical contexts, acknowledging the necessity of medicine while remaining critical. As Capstick and James Rupert Fletcher describe in their history of the field, 'dementia studies has moved from medicalisation to person-centred care to social citizenship and human rights-based approaches, with each of these "lenses" representing progress over time', but this sense of progress is also an oversimplification that they dispute amidst the complexity of what is known and not known about the dementia experience.[19] In this Element, I put dementia studies in conversation with Gothic studies, which subverts and devalues traditional notions of progress and has the potential to offer insights into how dementia narrative and identity might be interpreted, both of which impact cultural understandings and care of those with dementia.

1.2 The Gothic Approach: Accepting Fear and Confusion

One of the concerns shared amongst all dementia studies scholars is that of stereotyping and stigmatisation, and the Gothic and horror traditions have long been rightly implicated in these offenses. In leaning into excesses, the Gothic and horror twist and accentuate anxieties that already exist to the point of absurdity, which may deepen fears and lead to adverse behaviours and attitudes. It is widely thought that many marginalised groups represented by horror villains – people of different nationalities or races, misbehaving women, queer people, or unhoused people – can become targets for dehumanisation and abuse if people fear them. If audience members have had little interaction with people with mental illness, older people, or people with dementia, they may take these cultural representations – however hyperbolic – as representations of reality, applying the stigma they develop during the film or text to real-world figures. As Marlene Goldman writes, 'fiction, more than medicine, is responsible for shaping our concepts of disease': fiction becomes the strongest frame of reference, with very real consequences.[20]

This surface reading of horror may have some truth to it, but it obviously lacks nuance and is regularly disputed by moviegoers, creatives, and scholars. Stephen King has famously theorised an important purpose for horror: 'we make up horrors to help us cope with the real ones. With the endless inventiveness of humankind, we grasp the very elements which are so divisive and

---

[19] James Rupert Fletcher and Andrea Capstick, 'Introduction', in James Rupert Fletcher and Andrea Capstick (eds.), *A Critical History of Dementia Studies* (London: Routledge, 2024), pp. 1–9 (p. 2).

[20] Marlene Goldman, *Forgotten: Narratives of Age-Related Dementia and Alzheimer's Disease in Canada* (Chicago: McGill-Queen's University Press, 2017), p. 3.

destructive and try to turn them into tools – to dismantle themselves'.[21] He medicalises horror as 'the barber's leeches of the psyche, drawing not bad blood but anxiety', turning horror into a cure, not a disease.[22] We saw evidence of these theories in action when pandemic horror gained new popularity during the height of COVID-19, and some even claimed that horror fans exhibited particular resilience during this time of real medical horror.[23] Surviving a horror movie in the safety of a cinema or living room may give viewers the confidence to face other real-world fears that already exist. Psychologists, directly countering the narrative against horror, found that not only did horror *not* contribute to stigmatisation of mental illness through dehumanisation but it also actually improved viewers' perception of mental illness for two reasons: they saw monsters as 'atypical' representations of people with mental illness, and they recognised 'sympathetic qualities' in such 'monsters', sparking understanding and interest in medical conditions. As such, horror was deemed to 'provide some benefits in prejudice reduction'.[24] The excess and fakery that are mainstays of the Gothic and horror work in its favour by acknowledging underlying fears while reducing the reality of the monstrous threat. At the same time that horror vilifies characters considered to be outside the norm, it also champions such figures by making them central to the story and often complex and powerful. For modes that have often been dismissed, the Gothic and horror offer insights into anxieties impacted by prevailing cultural, political, and economic factors.

This quality of advocating for the Other is something the Gothic shares with horror and, as opposed to intensifying the otherworldly nature of the horrific as horror does, the Gothic quietly suggests that what is truly terrifying is found in a world indistinguishable from our own. This nuanced form of scare, then, provides closer access to experiences of dementia – though, those experiences are often extreme – by creating an intimacy between the viewer and the person with dementia. Because it dabbles with reality, the Gothic forces audiences to take a longer, more disturbing look at its fears. Though Gothic and horror often overlap, I do not use them interchangeably. If horror brings us into the film and then immediately out again with jump scares, the gothic draws us in more

---

[21] Stephen King, *Danse Macabre* (New York: Everest House, 1981), p. 26.
[22] King, *Danse Macabre*, p. 194.
[23] Coltan Scrivner, John A. Johnson, Jens Kjeldgaard-Christiansen, and Mathias Clasen, 'Pandemic Practice: Horror Fans and Morbidly Curious Individuals Are More Psychologically Resilient during the COVID-19 Pandemic', *Personality and Individual Differences*, 168 (2021): 1–6.
[24] Donald F. Sacco, Megan Walters, and Mitch Brown, 'Consumption of Psychological Horror Is Associated with Reduced Stigmatization of Mental Illness', *Journal of Media Psychology: Theories, Methods, and Applications* 37:3 (2024): 183–189 (p. 187).

slowly, more deviously, and is reluctant to let us go. Because of this subtlety, the Gothic is involved with the same concerns about stigmatisation and stereotyping but with, I would argue, even more occasion to flip that script. The Gothic may be more easily mistaken for reality, potentially villainising its subjects while also providing opportunities to expose and examine truths about horrors that actually exist. And it is not afraid to dig into the most gruesome and macabre ideas that disturb as much as scare.

I argue that the Gothic tradition's willingness to prioritise negative experiences of distress relating to physical and mental states is crucial for the understanding and improvement of healthcare. This is especially true for dementia, whose symptoms threaten the core of our place in the world and who we believe ourselves to be. While many texts about dementia want to uplift or move the audience, I would argue that the act of disturbing viewers also does important work. As Sara Wasson writes, 'Representations of intense distress are often seen as unhelpful by healthcare practitioners, medical humanities scholars, and disability studies scholars.... Yet prioritizing narratives with a positive slant can mean that some people's experience may be implicitly denigrated.'[25] There is more lost in denying troubling experiences than in dwelling on them. For example, Yoshizkaki-Gibbons notes that some films about dementia include the everyday distresses of 'care, financial, and social burdens',[26] which may not be fodder for jump scares but can nonetheless become real nightmare fuel. Prioritising negative experiences legitimises them, Gothic texts facilitating the act of witness and acknowledgement amongst its more outlandish themes.

Furthermore, most illnesses, injuries, and medical experiences involve some aspect of fear grounded in a loss of control over the body and its subsequent pain or humiliation. Mental and physical unwellness can cause us to fear one another, at the same time revealing our interdependence, not just for survival but for concepts of identity and selfhood. The field of health humanities benefits from the Gothic's continued reminder that medical experiences can be harrowing at the socio-political and biomedical levels, such that the health humanities – along with dementia studies and disability studies – remains timely and needed. Dementia, perhaps more than any other illness, demonstrates an area where fear of the disease itself and fear of those with the disease intersect, *despite* the fact that dementia is not contagious. Not only do those with dementia demonstrate fear alongside disorientation, memory loss, social isolation, and difficulty communicating, but even close family and friends may grow to fear someone

---

[25] Sara Wasson, *Transplantation Gothic: Tissue Transfer in Literature, Film, and Medicine* (Manchester: Manchester University Press, 2020), p. 24.

[26] Yoshizaki-Gibbons, 'Ageism and Ableism', p. 281.

with dementia becoming the heart-breaking combination of familiar and strange characteristic of Sigmund Freud's uncanny.[27] The Gothic illustrates and confronts these fears, providing opportunities to examine and interrogate, even while flirting with stigmatisation and stereotyping.

One of the most common points of distress for family and friends of those with dementia is the belief that they have become unrecognisable, that they have become uncanny. Their identity and familiar behaviours have shifted such that they seem like a completely different person because they would never do or say these things. But they *are* doing and saying these things. Changes in behaviour and speech may impact other core aspects of identity such as appearance, compounded with other challenges to memory and recognition. Interpreting this shift in identity as not just a change but also as a loss puts additional strain on relationships that are crucial to maintain for the emotional stability and health of both parties. This goes both ways: relationships also impact how changes in selfhood are navigated. Lisa Folkmarson Käll and Kristin Zeiler, in analysing the film *Still Alice* (Richard Glatzer and Wash Westmoreland, 2014), explain that subjectivity, rather than a static and vulnerable concept, is 'dynamic, relational, and continuously formed in relation with its surroundings and other people'.[28] As the environment and people change, so follows subjectivity, making its rigidity both impossible and undesirable.

Dementia studies, then, urges us to turn away from the deficit approach that characterises the medical model of disability and towards approaches that accept all humans as adapting and changing in ways that place them in and out of the 'norm' throughout their lives. It also prompts us to re-evaluate what selfhood comprises. Cultural texts like literature and film can respond to these questions, and the Gothic is well versed in questioning the status quo of selfhood more broadly. In looking at both fictional and biographical dementia narratives, Femi and Jan Oyebode point out that people with dementia maintain a sense of self through their use of language, even language that has become limited: 'they retain the capacity to use "I" phrases without difficulty ... they are never in doubt as to the fact that it refers to them', even if they become unsure of their own history and relationships. The I is an embodied self. Oyebode and Oyebode go on, 'Their relationship to their bodily parts is intact. They appreciate that their arms, legs, eyes, mouth are theirs.'[29] Thus, even if

---

[27] Sigmund Freud, *The Uncanny* (New York: Penguin, 2003).

[28] Lisa Folkmarson Käll and Kristin Zeiler, 'Still Alice?: Ethical Aspects of Conceptualising Selfhood in Dementia', in Alan Bleakley (ed.), *Routledge Handbook of the Medical Humanities* (London: Routledge, 2019), pp. 290–299 (p. 297).

[29] Femi Oyebode and Jan Oyebode, 'Personal Identity and Personhood: The Role of Fiction and Biographical Accounts in Dementia', in Tess Maginess (ed.), *Dementia and Literature: Interdisciplinary Perspectives* (London: Routledge, 2019), pp. 103–114 (p. 105).

they do not recognise those around them or if those around them find their behaviours out of character, their sense of individuality remains perhaps longer than even coherent language indicates. This distinguishes them from children, who do not yet have a sense of self from which to draw, despite the fact that people with dementia are often talked about and to as though they were children. Confusion does not necessarily equate to absence or undevelopment of selfhood, however, a point more difficult to see and believe the more language skills deteriorate.

This is where the Gothic can model fluctuating subjectivities and identities as well as reactions to them. In reframing the mechanics of identity, the Gothic teaches us not just to accept but to *expect* identity changes. Assumptions by those without dementia that new or different behaviours or speech patterns necessarily constitute a crisis are understandable, but Gothic reading strategies offer ways to reframe those changes, acknowledging loss while seeing beyond it. The Gothic primes readers to be suspicious of stable identities and to expect changes and challenges, and this trait is just one of a collective of conventions that resemble the dementia experience. From early texts like Horace Walpole's *The Castle of Otranto* (1764), the reader learns that characters are rarely what they seem, even to themselves. The protagonist Theodore begins the novel as an orphaned peasant but learns by the end that he is actually a prince with a living father, a change that impacts not just his socio-economic status but how he remembers his past, how that past has led to the present, and how completely different his future will be. It impacts his relationships and his environment, as well as his entire sense of who he thought he was. In more extreme examples, like Lord Byron's *The Deformed Transformed* (1824), the protagonist swaps bodies with a stranger, allowing him to become a different person, viewed differently and behaving differently because of it. Later Gothic examples like Robert Louis Stevenson's *Strange Case of Dr. Jekyll and Mr. Hyde* (1886) and stories by Edgar Allan Poe will destabilise identity for the individual even further by calling self-awareness and memory into question. Both involuntary and voluntary identity alternations occur throughout the Gothic tradition, promoting an expectation that identities can, do, even should change and that reliance on static identity is always doomed to fail. What is commonly identified as a deficiency is reframed as strength, one of many Gothic interpretive reversals.

1.3 Dementia Stories and Storytellers

Many discussions of dementia in literature and film tend towards didactic firsthand accounts filtered through third-party storytellers or sentimental tales of family struggle, lost romance, heroic perseverance, or rampant saviour complexes appeased on an individual or communal level. As Tess Maginess writes, literature reflects 'a reality with which we are familiar and a reality with which we are not familiar'.[30] Can narratives about dementia ever be anything but the latter for those who write it? Such narratives are inherently fraught by the necessity that those who produce them rarely have dementia themselves, even if they have first-hand medical or caregiving knowledge.[31] The notable exceptions tend to be personal memoirs chronicling the experience as it occurs, and these books are invaluable contributions to understanding the disease. When it comes to fiction, however, it is perhaps by necessity that writers must make assumptions and bring their own outsider status to depictions of dementia for readers who may also not have dementia. In fact, they may fear it. Disability scholars are rightfully sceptical of attempts to reproduce experiences so laden with stereotypes and stigma by those without first-hand experience. On the other hand, as Lucy Burke points out, in the service of intersubjectivity, if a person with dementia cannot tell their own story, it is doomed to remain untold unless those around them take it up and tell it however they can.[32] To lose that story may be worse than misrepresenting it. At the same time, narratives of dementia cannot help but participate in an 'us' versus 'them' dichotomy as they portray characters in conditions the author does not share, creating potential dangers in representation, even for authors with the best intentions.

Narratives that belittle: One common method for counteracting dehumanisation is garnering sympathy, but there is a fine line between sympathy and pity. Such narratives imply what a shame that a productive and fully functioning adult is reduced to helplessness by a brain disease. What a shame they have become a shell of their former self. What a shame that their families must now spend so much time, money, and effort to care for them amidst their own busy lives. As Yoshizaki-Gibbons writes of films like *What They Had* (2018) – whose tagline is 'A family united by the past. Divided by the present', which '[allows] the viewer to situate themselves within systems of compulsory youthfulness and compulsory able-bodiness/able-mindedness', relying heavily on ableist and ageist rhetorics of sentimentality to create feel-good affects. She adds, 'Care, particularly care for old disabled people, is rarely depicted as rewarding,

---

[30] Tess Maginess, 'Introduction', in Tess Maginess (ed.), *Dementia and Literature: Interdisciplinary Perspectives* (London: Routledge, 2018), pp. 1–20 (p. 10).

[31] Pieter Vermeulen, 'Infrastructures of Aging: Form and Institutional Care in Dementia Fiction', *Poetics Today* 44:1–2 (June 2023): 15–35 (p. 18).

[32] Lucy Burke, 'Missing Pieces: Trauma, Dementia and the Ethics of Reading in Elizabeth is Missing', in Tess Maginess (ed.), *Dementia and Literature: Interdisciplinary Perspectives* (London: Routledge, 2019), pp. 88–102 (p. 93).

fulfilling, or meaningful.'[33] Though it may also include experiences of love, compassion, and intimacy triggered by a diagnosis, the narrative becomes dominated by difficult decisions and sacrifice. The audience is encouraged to mourn the unsatisfied need to 'fix' the 'problem' of dementia and the burden the caregiver must now bear.

Narratives that blame: As nervous interest in preventing dementia has grown in media and culture, emphasis has fallen less on what science can do to provide preventative treatments and more on what individuals can do to stave off dementia through lifestyle changes. It is worth noting that self-help approaches to healthcare are nothing new and were seen as a form of empowerment in the eighteenth century, freeing individuals from relying on physicians. Today, in the age of medical bankruptcy, self-help might be read the same way. However, self-help rhetoric also makes prevention of dementia a matter of individual responsibility. Failure to achieve this goal implies personal weakness and the suggestion that negative consequences are deserved as punishment for lack of discipline. As Maginess points out, we see this rhetoric not just in fictional texts but also in the media.[34] Burke adds that narratives about dementia 'are intimately bound up with the meanings of family and care in a period in which structural transformations, "neoliberalisation" and, more recently austerity have placed intolerable pressures upon the capacity of people to support one another'.[35] As she notes, many of these texts focus on the impact of dementia on those involved without the disease: 'This often serves to re-inscribe the social marginalization of people with dementia',[36] despite, I would add, a probable need for caregiver narratives as they are undoubtedly part of the plot.

Narratives that assume: That the symptoms of dementia are largely centred around memory and communication creates obvious barriers to conventional storytelling, a situation explored in detail in Section 2. Despite this, Joan Rahilly argues that a person with dementia's use of 'non-standard language' does not necessarily mean that language is produced nonsensically. Rather, the rules differ from the standard rules of the listener or audience, which assume that no meaning can be made. How to preserve or convey this meaning, however, is the challenge. She writes, 'there would seem to be little benefit for writers in consistently replicating language such as this, which eludes understanding ... what we are left with is a comparatively ritualistic and formulaic approach to representing language in which only stereotypical features of language decline are evident'.[37] It is conventional storytelling that poses the problem here in its restricted capabilities: ill equipped to reflect the realistic communication of

---

[33] Yoshizaki-Gibbons, 'Ageism and Ableism', pp. 282, 284.   [34] Maginess, 'Introduction', p. 3.
[35] Burke, 'Missing Pieces', p. 88.   [36] Burke, 'Missing Pieces', p. 88.
[37] Rahilly, 'Language Breakdown', pp. 117–118.

a person with dementia – which must be conveyed by an outsider who is also ill-equipped to understand it – the alternative barely scratches the surface of a mind with dementia's complexity. This is where I suggest Gothic studies might add some perspective. Its 'incoherent' storytelling structures differ from what Rahilly describes because they're not trying to mimic dementia communication; they are already part of its foundations.

Negative reactions to people with dementia triggered by confused timelines, repetitive and fragmented communication, and inability to recall memories reveal that cultural understandings of dementia are just as obsessed with time as the Gothic is: an obsession with time as limited, linear, and 'accurate', however, rather than elastic, cyclical, and powerful. In combination with its excessive monsters and uncanny characters, I suggest that the narrative strategies that make the Gothic unique create a working context for culturally reframing dementia: in addition to unstable identities, unreliable narrators, fragmented storytelling, nonlinear narratives, unconventional chronologies, shifting character identities, unnatural lifespans, as well as hauntings, the uncanny, and the return of the repressed. These features resemble symptoms of dementia, but, though the Gothic has always been criticised for its reliance on 'cheap thrills', these features do not shut down readership as dementia symptoms interfere with relationships. Readers regularly encounter this collective of Gothic traits without assuming they indicate deficit. Instead, unconventional narrative structures are valued for the strengths they bring in building reader interest and involvement.

This Element offers new ways of conceptualising dementia and its place in creative work through the context of Gothic literature and Gothic techniques in horror film. I argue that the Gothic's narrative authorisation of unsettling and unstable styles, forms, aesthetics, images, and characters can be useful tools in navigating cultural understandings of dementia, which share similar traits. Across the Element's five sections, I demonstrate that the Gothic offers insight into dementia from two directions, (1) by relying on and therefore valuing the types of subversive and unsettling narrative and temporal manoeuvres that are considered problematic and therefore symptomatic in biomedical definitions of dementia (Sections 2 and 3) and (2) by modelling experiences of dementia through, albeit challenging, representations that reflect anxieties surrounding cognitive age-related illness like dementia (Sections 4 and 5).

While I advocate for new ways of thinking about and reacting to dementia in this Element, it is important to recognise that this disease poses significant emotional, financial, and practical challenges. In no way do I want to minimise or neglect the real trauma of the dementia experience for those who have it, their families, and others who care for them. My interest in this topic is informed by the lasting impact of pain and loss related to dementia in my own family. I argue that the Gothic is well suited to join this conversation because these horrors are real. My intention is not to judge or criticise the genuine struggles of many who are impacted by dementia. I am also not interested in diagnosing literary or film characters, particularly as I am speaking across historical time periods. Instead, I identify signs associated with dementia that share logic and affect with literary tropes and narrative techniques, some of which predate these medical concepts.

In Sections 2 and 3, I delve into fragmentation and nonlinear narrative techniques of foundational eighteenth- and nineteenth-century texts to reframe similar characteristics in dementia patients. With this, I suggest that Gothic reading strategies may open up possibilities for discovering meaning in dementia experience. In Section 3, I take on the convoluted perception of dementia as age-related while examining characters who live forever, questioning the desirability of this extreme wellness and the impact on the human (or superhuman) mind. In the second half of this Element, I confront the contentious depictions of characters with dementia in horror films to argue that, while guilty of reinforcing cultural understanding of dementia as horror and producing what disability studies calls 'narrative prosthesis' (the use of disabled characters as plot devices), these texts also usefully expose ways in which people with dementia are treated and the often hidden aspects of the disease from different points of view.[38] In Sections 4 and 5, I examine horror films explicitly about characters exhibiting clear symptoms of dementia to untangle Gothic elements in both the medical space (Section 4) and the home (Section 5). In Section 4, I explore how the supernatural reveals the dangerous power of a dementia diagnosis to redefine one's identity. In Section 5, I examine films that downplay the supernatural and redefine relationships in disturbing, but necessary, ways that extend the dementia experience to family carers. In introducing Gothic literature and horror film as valuable lenses through which to critically consider the ways we think about dementia, I hope this Element opens up opportunities for the Gothic to be seen as more than just a problematic generator of stigma and for literary studies more broadly to have a larger role in dementia studies.

2 Cycles of Fear: Fragmentation and Temporal Confusion

The infrequent inclusion of the Gothic in dementia studies is surprising because its very form mimics culturally recognised symptoms of the disease. Mimic, however, is an inaccurate term as mimicry suggests that one intentionally resembles the other in a way that implies inferiority: neither is true in this

---

[38] David T. Mitchell and Sharon L. Snyder, *Narrative Prosthesis: Disability and the Dependencies of Discourse* (Ann Arbor: University of Michigan Press, 2001).

case. The texts discussed in this section differ from the typical approach to dementia and literature in that they do not feature characters diagnosed with dementia and do not necessarily include characters exhibiting its symptoms. Rather, this section considers Gothic genric forms and storytelling methods that challenge conventional narrative structures, such as identity alterations, repetition and fragments. In forcing readers to traverse fragmentation, uncanny temporalities, conflicting stories and nonlinear chronologies, the Gothic models interpretive strategies that may carry over to nonnormative narratives outside the safe spheres of literature and film. If dementia is seen as an illness that hinders memory and communication, then the Gothic's predilection for incapacitating conventional stories in similar ways is well positioned to train agile readers who can cope with incompleteness.

From the first Gothic novel, Horace Walpole's *The Castle of Otranto* (1764), characters struggle to gain coherent information from the rambling nonsensical characters who witness supernatural events, such characters being literally scared silly and discounted as useless. This absence of comprehensible information or dialogue results in a useless interaction, or so the villain thinks. Similarly, as Susanne Katharina Christ says of these qualities in dementia patients, 'An illness that fundamentally impacts on self-determined living, productivity, cognitive functioning, and communication poses a deep threat to values held dear by twenty-first century Western societies'.[39] As Stephen Katz and Annette Leibing add, this assumption that the dementia experience is fraught with fragmentation is 'due to the historical construction of Euro-Western concepts of personhood itself, characterised by certainty, rationality, agency, memory and individuality'.[40] Margaret Oldfield and Nancy Hansen add that 'Western society tends to overvalue cognitive intelligence and thereby undervalue the contributions of people with cognitive impairments'.[41] But the Gothic has a long history of elevating repetitive or fragmented narratives to a primary form of meaning-making, disrupting many of these concepts in the process. Gothic texts of the eighteenth and nineteenth centuries – centuries that arguably developed the values Katz and Leibing list – tell their stories in fragments, gaps, and cycles that question the value of clear selfhood and Enlightenment progress. I argue that the same interpretive strategies adopted by readers of these texts might model ways of reframing and approaching

---

[39] Susanne Katharina Christ, *Fictions of Dementia: Narrative Modes of Presenting Dementia in Anglophone Novels* (Berlin: De Gruyter, 2022), p. 4.
[40] Katz and Leibing, '"Lost in Time"', p. 57.
[41] Margaret Oldfield and Nancy Hansen, 'Power, Agency, Aging, and Cognitive Impairment', in Katie Aubrecht, Christine Kelly, and Carla Rice (eds.), *The Aging-Disability Nexus* (Toronto: UBC, 2020), pp. 130–144 (p. 132).

dementia symptoms and those who exhibit them as fully capable of making valuable meaning, even if that meaning is unconventional. Gothic texts intentionally swap or alter character identities, withhold information, repeat things, disrupt story chronologies, and leave narratives unfinished knowing that readers will suspend confusion, frustration, or judgement to successfully access meaning.

2.1 Shifting Identities and Perspectives

Arguably, changes in identity can be the most alarming and isolating of dementia's symptoms: fluctuations in mood, increased frustration with growing confusion, actions that are irrational or violent can scare caring witnesses. An inability to recognise family or community members means that shifting identities might go both ways, individuals with dementia and family members feeling threatened by sudden 'strangers', threats that will be explored more in Sections 4 and 5. The foreignness of altered identities can cause dehumanisation, dismissal, and abuse against which individuals with dementia cannot defend themselves. All approaches within dementia studies aim to call attention to and alleviate these difficulties, regardless of disagreements about how. A major component of this aim is recognising the importance of stories – those told by, about, and to individuals with dementia – as crucial for navigating identity shifts.

Stories are central to notions of selfhood, and those stories involve – or should involve – the notion of a life lived prior to a dementia diagnosis that takes into account past experiences felt on both individual and systemic levels. While efforts to access, reproduce, and preserve the stories of those with dementia can provide a fuller understanding of who they have been and who they have become, there are also dangers in misinterpreting those stories.[42] Andrea Capstick argues against what she calls a 'dehistoricised' view of dementia that neglects the story already in progress, akin to what Arthur W. Frank discusses as 'Narrative Wreck' for a life course that has been narratively shipwrecked by illness and needs to be remapped.[43] Getting lost in narrative can be disorienting for anyone who is ill and their caregivers. Capstick advocates for 'a recognition (at minimum) that the socioeconomic conditions prevailing throughout a person's life, the periods of history they have

---

[42] Jackie Kindell, Aagje Swinnen, and John Keady, '"Whose Story Is It and What Is It For?": Life Story as Critical Discourse in Dementia Studies', in James Rupert Fletcher and Andrea Capstick (eds.), *A Critical History of Dementia Studies* (London: Routledge, 2024), pp. 125–137 (pp. 125, 135).

[43] Capstick, 'The Century', p. 27; Arthur W. Frank, *The Wounded Storyteller: Body, Illness, and Ethics*, 2nd Ed. (Chicago: University of Chicago Press, 1997), p. 54.

lived through, and the impact of internalised social mores belonging to those periods are all important influences in later life'.[44] These past experiences may encroach on a timeline later in life in unexpected ways that, to a mind navigating changes in memory and communication, manifest as symptoms. Here, the Gothic notion of the past as powerful, even if unknown or unacknowledged according to Freud's concept of the return of the repressed, may be useful reminders that someone with dementia is continually shaped by their past, even if unable to consciously recall it in coherent fashion.

As mentioned in Section 1, characters in Gothic narratives are rarely who they appear to be, even to themselves. These new forms are not divorced from the past, though they may promote new interpretations of that past and changes to expectations of the future. In some instances, characters physically change into another person or an inhuman figure; in others, identity changes through narrative alone, a rewriting of some of the socio-economic factors mentioned by Capstick. Matthew Lewis's infamous 1796 novel *The Monk* features characters of both types: The devoted religious novice Rosario reveals herself to be Matilda, a female enchantress in disguise, who manipulates the title character Ambrosio into corruption and despair, an alteration of the public persona of power through purity. Matilda resembles the portrait of the Madonna that hangs in Ambrosio's room, which she claims to have had painted in her likeness for him. At the end of the novel, however, she has shapeshifted once again into Satan himself. In addition to his dual identities as saint by day and sinner by night, Ambrosio's identity also further changes when he learns that he is the son of a woman he murdered and the brother of a woman he raped, his identity traumatically rewritten and aligned with women he previously considered strangers. Within the foundation of formulaic tropes, identity is reliably unreliable in these early Gothic tales.

Readers of the Gothic expect these surprise shifts in identity as important plot twists, so much so that characters who embrace the other extreme, total and utter stability of identity, are unusual and unsettling. The most infamous example of an attempt at an unchanging identity is Miss Havisham in Charles Dickens's *Great Expectations* (1861), a character whose only growth is age and decay. Miss Havisham paused her life on her wedding day, when she was abandoned by her fiancé. While the wedding clothes yellow and the feast rots, her physical body ages and her identity alters in the sense that she once was defined by her future marital bliss. Preoccupied with its loss, she has become one without a future, whose past has engulfed her. Protagonist Pip notes the inevitable change when he sees 'the bride within the bridal dress had withered like the

---

[44] Capstick, 'The Century', p. 27.

dress, and like the flowers, and had no brightness left but the brightness of her sunken eyes', comparing her to both a waxwork and a skeleton.[45] Thus, even characters who attempt to preserve themselves and their surroundings find that relying on absolute rigidity of identity is doomed to fail.

2.2 Repetition and Memory Loss: When Time Gets Stuck

Miss Havisham attempts to stop time at a point where joy meets trauma, protecting herself from the consequences of abandonment by refusing to create any new experiences, starting with her immediate experience of embodiment: changing her clothes or altering the environment, both of which alter anyway. She exhibits a Gothic preoccupation with the past and an inability to distinguish that past from the present or future. Though Dickens's character seems to suffer more from stubbornness than genuine belief in this delusion, she introduces typical symptoms of dementia into the narrative: confusion about the passage of time that may lead to repetition or dwelling in the past. Difficulty with memory (especially short-term memory) is an early-stage indicator of dementia. Struggles to express these memories – a loss of language – may indicate a shift to a later stage.[46] This disruption of linear narrative production then becomes central to stories about dementia. Christ describes it as 'defined by temporal changes in spontaneous speech, problems with word finding and word retrieval, phonemic and semantic paraphasia, reduced syntactic complexity, reduction in productive and receptive discourse-level processing and many other elements'.[47] Replicating these types of communication deviations accurately, however, may sabotage a narrative's ability to reach readers, and some dementia studies scholars point to problematic assumptions made in such portrayals. Jackie Kindell, Aagje Swinnen, and John Keady point out that narratives of memory loss inspire a move to 'repair' the memory through repetitive correction. They worry that narratives intentionally replicating dementia traits might pass on such feelings of deficit and brokenness, confirming interpretations that promote 'fixing' a narrator rather than adapting to the narration.[48] Pieter Vermeulen articulates similar concerns held by dementia scholars that replicating symptoms through literature may result in contrived and patronising imitations of narrative lack that '[risk] misrecognizing the lives it putatively wants to elevate', and he targets the personhood approach to dementia, discussed more in Section 5.[49]

In other words, as narratives attempting to reproduce the cognitive and communicative experience of dementia are almost always written by authors

---

[45] Charles Dickens, *Great Expectations* (New York: Signet Classic, 1980), p. 67.
[46] Joan Rahilly, 'Language Breakdown', p. 116.   [47] Christ, *Fictions of Dementia*, p. 25.
[48] Kindell, Swinnen, and Keady, '"Whose Story Is It"', p. 135.
[49] Vermeulen, 'Infrastructures of Aging', p. 18.

without dementia or writers in the early stages of dementia, those narratives will always be somewhat removed from their subjects and rely on observation and assumption rather than experience. As Christ writes, 'Narrating dementia means narrating the inability to narrate': its very premise makes it impossible as it relies on what it cannot have.[50] Naomi Kruger adds that not only can such productions be inaccurate and stereotypical, but they can also have dangerous impacts on cultural attitudes towards dementia that diminish care.[51] For these reasons, I actively avoid texts with these intentions in this Element. The Gothic introduces an alternative approach to these debates between literary studies and dementia studies. Vermeulen cautions that 'tying the imagining of dementia to formlessness either surrenders it to cultural anxieties ... or, alternatively, invites inflating the mental state that marks dementia into a form of visionary and prophetic insight', two misrepresentations that disability studies scholars might recognise as familiar and reductive depictions of disability in popular culture.[52] None of these readings see formlessness as a form of meaning in itself.

Gothic texts do, and their approaches to time, memory, and form are already similar to dementia symptoms without intentionally imitating them. The very spaces in which Gothic texts are set are anchored to the past: cemeteries, ancient castles, old ruins, ancestral lands. History built into the space impacts the minds and behaviours of the characters trapped within it, creating repetitive acts and confused identities as new memories resemble the old. For example, Emily Bronte's *Wuthering Heights* (1847) is restricted to two houses and the land between them, forming a microcosm of doubled characters who share the same names, same eyes, same traumas in a cycle of abuse that sees movement in time but no progress. Heathcliff detains Catherine in order to possess her deceased mother of the same name, an impossible task that seems achievable in a space where she once lived. Time can be crossed again and again in these unchanging spaces that indefinitely delay the future for its captives.

With time and space equally ever-present and inconsistent, Gothic narratives affect the reader as much as the characters, culminating in nonlinear storytelling akin to the nonlinearity of dementia communication. Both pose challenges to audiences expecting conventional coherent narratives. Steven Willemsen and Miklós Kiss ask, 'what makes nonlinear narratives cognitively demanding ... what real-world cognitive abilities allow spectators to engage with a story's

---

[50] Christ, *Fictions of Dementia*, p. 29.
[51] Naomi Kruger, 'The "Terrifying Question Mark": Dementia, Fiction, and the Possibilities of Narrative', in Aagje Swinnen and Mark Schweda (eds.), *Popularizing Dementia: Public Expressions and Representations of Forgetfulness* (Bielefeld: Transcript, 2015), pp. 109–136 (p. 109).
[52] Vermeulen, 'Infrastructures of Aging', pp. 19–20.

challenging deviations from everyday temporality?'[53] I ask in response, can the methods through which we navigate nonnormative storytelling techniques in cultural texts apply to dementia communication? Gothic readers are particularly well versed in negotiating meandering, nonsequential, repetitive, and fragmented stories and are proficient in Samuel Taylor Coleridge's concept of 'suspension of disbelief', a trust and willingness to put aside conventional world restrictions, to accept changes as they occur without losing the thread of character identity or story, 'which constitutes poetic faith'.[54] Some might interpret dementia symptoms as 'wandering, incoherence, or non-compliance', all showcased in the Gothic, which respects the wanderer, expects incoherence, and sees non-compliance as a creative strength.[55] In part, these skills originated with the Romantics like Coleridge, who made incompleteness and confusion into an art.

In part, these qualities of the Gothic grew out of the literary experimentation of Romantic writers more broadly, even those who did not intentionally participate in the Gothic tradition. Writers like William Wordsworth and Coleridge saw memory as central to the power of imagination, combining new understandings of individuality with interrogations of time and meditations on space. Wordsworth is well known for acknowledging identities that evolve over the years, grounded in spaces that preserve time. Seeking out past versions of himself in 'Lines Composed a Few Miles Above Tintern Abbey' (1798) and revisiting places that are temporal as well as geographic, he describes 'spots of time' marking emotionally significant occurrences rooted in place and collapsing the past and the present through his many revisions of his autobiographical *The Prelude* (1805).[56] In anchoring time in these physical areas, he introduces the malleability and accessibility of certain memories that can be mentally returned to just as a place is physically revisited. A spot also indicates a physical mark remaining from a past event that may fade with time but nonetheless persists. As Wordsworth returns to these spots of time for familiarity, comfort, and relief, dementia patients revert back to impactful times in their lives, getting stuck in a spot that is meaningful to them. Capstick reminds us that past events that occurred 'between approximately 5 and 30 years of age often

---

[53] Steven Willemsen and Miklós Kiss, 'Keeping Track of Time: The Role of Spatial and Embodied Cognition in the Comprehension of Nonlinear Storyworlds', *Style* 54:2 (2020): 172–198 (p. 173).
[54] Samuel Taylor Coleridge, 'Biographia Literaria; or Biographical Sketches of my Literary Life and Opinions', in Joseph Black, Leonard Conolly, Kate Flint et al. (eds.), *The Broadview Anthology of Romantic Poetry* (Peterborough: Broadview Press, 2016), pp. 560–573 (p. 567).
[55] Katz and Leibing, '"Lost in Time"', p. 62.
[56] William Wordsworth, 'The Prelude: Book XI', in Stephen Gill (ed.), *William Wordsworth: The Major Works* (Oxford: Oxford World's Classics, 2000), pp. 559–568 (p. 565).

Gothic Dementia 21

[remain] intact when short-term memory becomes compromised'.[57] Thus, dementia communication may be inspired by cycles of personal history, returning to the same spots over and over, caught in repetition that returns to a spot of time in the space of the mind rather than in nature.

Others like Coleridge document the elusiveness of even recent memory by acknowledging the impact of forgetting in his poem, 'Kubla Khan; Or, A Vision in a Dream. A Fragment' (1816), to which he adds a note about the circumstances in which it was written. Waking from a drug-induced dream of having composed it, he writes of himself, 'if that indeed can be called composition in which all the images rose up before him as things, with a parallel production of the correspondent expressions, without any sensation or consciousness of effort'.[58] He quickly copies down the lines as he remembers them from his dream but is called away for an hour and, 'found, to his no small surprise and mortification, that though he still retained some vague and dim recollection of the general purport of the vision, yet, with the exception of some eight or ten scattered lines and images, all the rest had passed away', resulting in one of Coleridge's most cryptic and captivating poems.[59] 'Kubla Khan' defies coherence and demands that readers find creative methods to traverse its vague and often contradictory depictions of interrupted time and dreamlike space, full of characters whose past, present, and future are matters of confusion amidst anxieties about forgetfulness and loss. Any expectation of linear narrative here will be disappointed. And yet, it is a poem of endless critical interest, meaning, and enjoyment.

2.3 Fragments: Gaps and Insufficient Language

Coleridge calls his poem 'A fragment'. Though he goes out of his way to emphasise the incompleteness of it, fragments more generally speaking are considered to be complete and valid pieces of artistic expression for the Romantics amongst whom they were popular. Yet, fragments and fragmentation of thought, memory, or narrative are seen as symptoms of decline within the context of dementia, where it may be used to discredit or disengage from attempts at communication. Tied to incompleteness, formlessness, disorientation, and incapacity, fragmentation makes a speaker unreliable because they appear unanchored, unaware of who, where, or when they are and incapable of understanding their surroundings. To family and friends, these symptoms may

---

[57] Capstick, 'The Century', p. 31.
[58] Samuel Taylor Coleridge, 'Kubla Khan, Or, A Vision in a Dream: A Fragment', Joseph Black, Leonard Conolly, Kate Flint et al. (eds.), *The Broadview Anthology of Romantic Poetry* (Peterborough: Broadview Press, 2016), pp. 556–557 (p. 556).
[59] Coleridge, 'Kubla Khan', p. 556.

also make someone with dementia seem foreign, even inhuman, interacting with the world and others in ways unlike they have in the past. This can be particularly upsetting if those around them rely on their stable identity.

Christine Bryden, who calls herself a 'dementia survivor' after being diagnosed at age forty-six, has written of her experience, defying medical expectations and offering invaluable first-hand insights. She talks about the fear of memory loss and needing help to understand the past, while also questioning the necessity of that fear: 'this assumes that my sense of being an embodied self is dependent on recalling what I did, rather than on knowing who I am'.[60] In other words, the present self's access to the past self should not determine the legitimacy of any of these temporal selves. She further remarks that 'a robot could be programmed to recall accurately the entire record of its "life", yet it cannot be regarded to know what it is or to have a sense of meaning'.[61] The implication is that once an individual exhibits difficulty communicating (early stage) or a lack of any communication (late stage), they forfeit their status as a person.[62] Because of the inability to form coherent, chronological communication, people with dementia are dismissed as incapable of making meaning or having meaningful lives and, therefore, are discountable.[63] Dementia studies scholars work to expose and deter these reductive attitudes, questioning whom that communication is actually for. In valuing communication without completeness, Gothic fragments redirect attention from the product of meaning (the completed, whole work) to the process of making meaning without coherent past or future, of existing only in the current diegetic moment.

The eighteenth- and nineteenth-century appreciation of narrative fragments is assisted by the period's growing interest in architectural ruins and in the anachronistic, contrived plots of the Gothic. At the same time, Anne Janowitz reminds us that a fragment is not necessarily a ruin: 'If something is ruined, then presumably it once had a full form that has eroded through time. A fragment, on the other hand, is simply part of a whole', and it is true that many fragments discussed next are simply left unfinished, intentionally or not.[64] But, fragmented narratives in the Gothic may also be *simulated* ruins, pieces of narrative that imply the loss of the whole through neglect or time, when in fact that lost whole has never existed. Loss and fragmentation in the Gothic are ultimately fabricated or counterfeit and encourage the reader to increase their own

---

[60] Christine Bryden, *Will I Still Be Me? Finding a Continuing Sense of Self in the Lived Experience of Dementia* (London: Jessica Kingsley, 2018), p. 67.
[61] Bryden, *Will I Still*, p. 67.   [62] Rahilly, 'Language Breakdown', p. 116.
[63] Kruger, 'The "Terrifying Question Mark"', p. 109.
[64] Anne Janowitz, 'The Romantic Fragment', in Duncan Wu (ed.), *A Companion to Romanticism* (Oxford: Blackwell, 2017), pp. 479–488 (p. 481).

involvement in the story by compelling them to fill in the gaps and navigate incompleteness with ease. Not only is the Gothic fragment enough to convey significant meaning, as Levinson describes, but 'its success would be of a different kind, or greatly diminished, or entirely obstructed were anything added to it'.[65] Fragmented narratives like bits of letters or scraps of ancient text found within complete Gothic works legitimise those texts by suggesting a natural (or supernatural) impact of time on a physical artefact, manuscript, or letter. Documents missing pieces add realism despite their obvious fakery. To finish a fragment, Gothic or otherwise, would ironically be to *ruin* it. One of the best-known examples, 'Sir Bertrand, A Fragment',[66] begins with the words, ' – After this adventure' but gives no hints to access that previous adventure and ends with 'addressed him in these words:—' without providing those words or what comes next.[67] Nothing comes next because there is no next.

Thus, the fragment gestures towards potential missing material that does not exist: there is a past and a future for these characters, but at the same time there is not. This speaks to a reframing of incompleteness as a form of completeness not unlike Bryden's insistence that the absence of complete memory does not indicate an absence of legitimate present, nor a lack of self-awareness for those with dementia. Similarly, Vermeulen insists that the dementia experience is 'a full-fledged form', despite its appearance as discombobulated or missing pieces.[68] While the missing material of the dementia experience *did* at one point exist, it may not exist at that moment for that speaker. The Gothic's withholding of complete information is what ignites rather than shuts down acts of narrative discovery, allowing for an unlimited expansion of the story that exists in mere suggestion and conjecture. Sophie Thomas intimates that the fragment itself is even downright creepy, that 'fragments are, by definition, disturbing entities. They play upon the imagination by promising or suggesting more than what they are, while reminding the viewer or reader that what they promise can never be recovered or fully experienced'.[69] The withholding of information is part of the Gothic's agenda for withholding comfort, certainty, and safety, even as its predictable and repetitive tropes produce those same qualities. It forces readers to work with what they have.

---

[65] Marjorie Levinson, *The Romantic Fragment Poem: A Critique of a Form* (Chapel Hill: The University of North Carolina Press, 1986), p. 7.
[66] Some attribute this fragment to Anna Laetitia Barbauld while others cite her brother, John Aiken.
[67] John Aiken and Anna Letitia Barbauld, 'Sir Bertrand, A Fragment', in E. J. Clery and Robert Miles (eds.), *Gothic Documents: A Sourcebook, 1700–1820* (Manchester: Manchester University Press, 2000), pp. 130–132.
[68] Vermeulen, 'Infrastructures of Ageing', p. 24.
[69] Sophie Thomas, 'The Fragment', in Nicholas Roe (ed.), *Romanticism: An Oxford Guide* (Oxford: Oxford University Press 2005), pp. 502–519 (p. 502).

While some fragments – like 'Sir Bertrand' – are published independently, others may be found subsumed into whole texts they don't belong to, chopped up and repurposed, rewritten for different aims, not unlike memories that get misplaced in other memories or confusions about the current time and place. Even though it may seem like a perfectly preserved moment in time, the fragment is no more stable than a Gothic identity or a human memory, regardless of the rememberer's dementia status. Kirstin A. Mills refers to the cannibalism of this type of reuse and abuse of fragments in versions of Gottfried August Bürger's ballad 'Lenore', all of which 'remain haunted by the spectres of their past forms, rendering the process of reading and writing "Lenore" in the late eighteenth and nineteenth centuries a gothic spectral conjuring'.[70] Thus, what Mills implies is that, alongside the popularity of the Romantic fragment, the Gothic is also a vehicle for these types of repurposed or relocated narrative pieces, their cyclical use raising the dead by taking it out of one context and transplanting it into another until it becomes part of a jumble of narrative pieces. We see this in the work of Matthew Lewis, who was frequently accused of plagiarising the work of German poets like Bürger, but recycling, duplication, and fragmentation also occur in reductions of multi-volume novels into short chapbooks. Lewis's plot about Raymond and Agnes in *The Monk* (1796) is fragmented from the original, given new character names, and published as the 44-page *Almagro & Claude; or Monastic Murder; Exemplified in the Dreadful Doom of an Unfortunate Nun* (1803), as well as appearing in several other chapbooks in a similar fashion. Part of the appeal of the Gothic for readers is the comforting and recognisable repetition of its tropes and conventions. Discovering a familiar fragment calls attention to not just a recycling of plots but an interrupted or repeated reading event that may recall prior reading experiences, collapsing time for the reader and inducing a reading network made up of layered and atemporal experiences. Reencountering texts, like reencountering memories, may not necessarily replicate the exact experience of the original. Kindell, Swinnen, and Keady describe remembering as 'not a static, once-only event. It is an interactional experience that moves through and over time creating multiple life storylines in the process'.[71] Encounters with the Romantic Gothic fragment, then, promote this multiplicity of narrative pieces that are just as effective at moving the reader as any conventional beginning-to-end text.

Gothic fragmented narratives may disorient the reader by creating the uncanny feeling of cyclical incompleteness, but they may also demonstrate

---

[70] Kirstin A. Mills, 'Haunted by "Lenore": The Fragment as Gothic Form, Creative Practice and Textual Evolution', *Gothic Studies* 23.2 (2021): 132–147 (p. 133).

[71] Kindell, Swinnen, and Keady, '"Whose Story Is It"', p. 132.

the inadequacy of linguistic communication and its dangers. Incoherent communication and temporality can shield readers from horrific experiences by delivering them indirectly in emotional piecemeal. To protect the reader from forbidden, potentially self-annihilating information or to convey the ineffability and inexpressibility of human experience: both goals materialise as fragment. We see repeated instances of fragments signified by visual gaps that forego language altogether in Charles Maturin's meandering and cyclical novel, *Melmoth the Wanderer* (1820), including multiple rows of asterisks that mark sections of found manuscripts that are illegible or missing. Significant gaps also precede conversations between the title character and the manuscript writer Stanton, as well as em dashes chopping up their stilted conversation: For example, '"You were in question of me?" – "I was." "Have you anything to inquire of me?" – "Much." "Speak, then" – "This is no place"', blending the two sides of the conversation into one pile of fragments shared by both.[72] A later moment circumvents any type of conventional communication by replacing both words and asterisks with sheet music, shown in Figures 1(a) and 1(b). These gaps and fragments gesture towards a futility of chronological time and coherent language characteristic of the character, Melmoth, whose very presence interferes with comprehensible communication and temporality. He will be further discussed in Section 3.

These types of gaps also mimic authorial interruption like Coleridge's lost train of thought or, more tragically, unfinished manuscripts left by writers upon death. Mary Wollstonecraft's unfinished Gothic novel, *Maria; Or, the Wrongs of Woman* (published posthumously in 1798) ends with a series of fragments conveying her ideas about possible storylines and endings for her novel about a woman committed to an asylum by her corrupt husband. Wollstonecraft's own husband William Godwin includes a note 'By the Editor' that explains the 'very few hints respecting the plan for the remainder of the work. I find only two detached sentences, and some scattered heads for the continuation of the story. I transcribe the whole', 'whole' indicating that these fragments, though incomplete, do not indicate the existence of missing pieces.[73] Any speculation about the gaps between the drafted narrative and these fragments cannot be confirmed, leaving the reader to negotiate incomplete information using their own powers of interpretation. Two of the fragments contain fully developed concepts, but the 'scattered heads' resemble the conversation between Stanton and Melmoth with their use of em-dashes and lack of details: 'A prosecution for adultery commenced—Trial—Darnford sets out for France—Letters—Once

---

[72] Charles Maturin, *Melmoth the Wanderer* (Oxford: Oxford World's Classics, 1989), p. 44.
[73] Mary Wollstonecraft, *Maria; Or, the Wrongs of Woman*, edited by Anne K. Mellor (New York: W.W. Norton, 1994), p. 135.

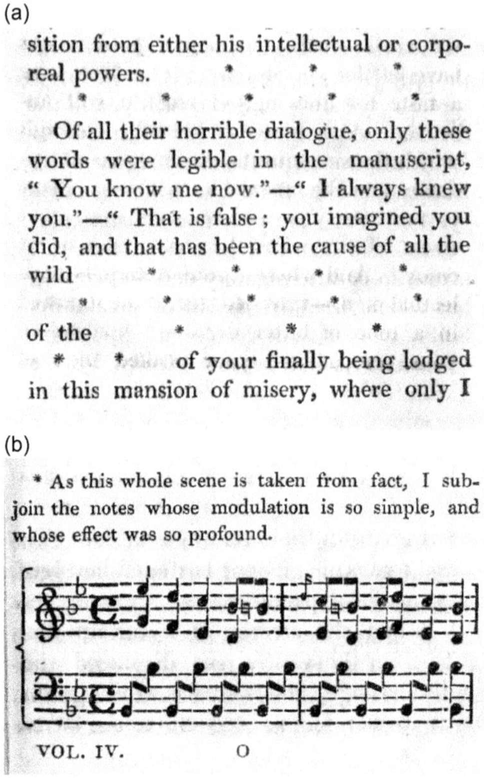

(a)

sition from either his intellectual or corporeal powers.   *   *   *
*   *   *   *   *

Of all their horrible dialogue, only these words were legible in the manuscript, " You know me now."—" I always knew you."—" That is false; you imagined you did, and that has been the cause of all the wild   *   *   *   *
*   *   *   *   *
of the   *   *   *
*   *   of your finally being lodged in this mansion of misery, where only I

(b)

* As this whole scene is taken from fact, I subjoin the notes whose modulation is so simple, and whose effect was so profound.

VOL. IV.   O

Figure 1 (a) Gaps and nonverbal forms of communication in *Melmoth the Wanderer*.

Source: Charles Maturin, *Melmoth the Wanderer* (Edinburgh: Archibald Constable & Co., 1820), p. 132. https://hdl.handle.net/2027/dul1.ark:/13960/t80k3pk0w
(b) Gaps and nonverbal forms of communication in Melmoth the Wanderer.

Source: Charles Maturin, *Melmoth the Wanderer* (Edinburgh: Archibald Constable & Co., 1820), p. 313. https://hdl.handle.net/2027/dul1.ark:/13960/t2s480129

more pregnant—He returns—Mysterious behaviour—Visit—Expectation—Discovery—Interview—Consequence.'[74] While a reader might flounder in the disorientation of gaps, fragments, and ambiguity left in these notes, *Maria* is not taken less seriously because of them. Some might argue that the unfinished insights into Wollstonecraft's creative process are more likely to engage reader curiosity and interpretation. Fragmented texts, in these senses, suffer no lack of meaning or relevance.

Godwin does not attempt to organise or add commentary to Wollstonecraft's fragments, leaving them complete in their incompleteness. This counters the

---

[74] Wollstonecraft, *Maria*, p. 136.

anxieties demonstrated by some other writers of the time to rework their text through different editions, combining the instability of narrative identity with worries about coherence and reader interpretation. In a stark turn from his writing of 'Kubla Khan', Coleridge's *The Rime of the Ancient Mariner* (originally *The Rime of the Ancyent Marinere*) went through at least eighteen identity shifts throughout its publication history, including changes in spelling and new and cut content.[75] The marginal gloss added to the 1817 version attempts to clear up any potential confusions in the main poem by providing interpretation, but it does so using archaic language that harkens back to that earlier version. For example, the marginal note for the lines, '"Why look'st thou so?" – With my cross-bow/ I shot the ALBATROSS', reads, 'The ancient Mariner inhospitably killeth the pious bird of good omen.'[76] While this poem will be discussed more in the next section, it is worth noting that it features all of the signs of dementia communication discussed here: unstable identity, cyclical and fragmented narratives, and a compulsion for telling uncontrollable stories. The 1798 version includes frequent repetition of phrases, such as 'There was a ship' and 'Alone, alone, all all alone/Alone on the wide wide Sea', perhaps precipitated by listener interruptions or the speaker losing his train of thought.[77] While dementia is thought of as a cognitive disease, efforts to retrieve lost language or memories may register as physical discomfort. Though the Mariner has a captive audience, his story includes moments when he physically cannot speak or feels divorced from his own powers of communication: 'I quak'd to think of my own voice/ How frightful it would be!'[78] The act of repeatedly telling his story, of participating in a cycle of unwinding narrative, likewise has a physical effect. In the 1798 version, a 'woeful agony' forces him to begin the cycle anew, and in the 1817 version, his heart 'burns' until the story is told, intimating that repetition will continue as long as he lives.[79]

The ways in which the Mariner returns to the past, gets lost in narrative, struggles to communicate and speaks in fragments – even Coleridge's attempt to speak for him through the 1817 gloss – are all classic Gothic narrative manoeuvres and are also akin to dementia behaviours and reactions. Thomas claims that the fragmented narrative 'undermines the distinctions that criticism depends on, such as a clear sense of the limits and borders of texts'.[80] In other words, it necessitates alternate, unconventional ways to evaluate its potential for

---

[75] Jack Stillinger, 'The Multiple Versions of Coleridge's Poems: How Many "Mariners" Did Coleridge Write?' *Studies in Romanticism* 31:2 (Summer 1992): 127–146 (p. 127).
[76] Samuel Taylor Coleridge, *The Rime of the Ancient Mariner*, edited by Paul H. Fry (Boston: Bedford/St. Martin's, 1999), p. 33.
[77] Coleridge, *The Rime*, pp. 28, 46.   [78] Coleridge, *The Rime*, p. 54.
[79] Coleridge, *The Rime*, pp. 72–73.   [80] Thomas, 'The Fragment', p. 512.

meaning. While the listener originally dismisses the Mariner as unworthy of attention, he also reveals the power of this Gothic narrative through his inability to escape it, despite the obvious discomfort and fear he experiences in the older man's presence. The act of listening changes him, making him 'sadder and wiser', providing yet more evidence of the impact and value of unconventional stories.[81]

As this section has demonstrated, the types of unstable identities, cyclical narratives, gaps, and fragments that inspire infantilisation or dehumanisation of an individual when read as symptoms of dementia are prevalent in Romantic and Gothic literature, to which readers do not react with similar dismissal but rather find creative and critical methods to navigate and create meaning. I suggest that Gothic appreciation of inconsistency might model a reframing of dementia symptoms in ways that lessen deteriorations in human connection through fear caused by lost communication and shifts in identity. Bryden asks, 'Why should the ability to retain memories be regarded as so critical to having a sense of self? Why should a lack of accurate and reliable recall of past events mean I am losing myself?'[82] Adhering to expectations of linear, complete narrative implies recognition of only one type of chronological coherence as a legitimate method of making meaning. Gothic literature demonstrates that readers and listeners are not just capable of, but *skilled* at navigating unconventional literary narratives, a skill that might be applicable in the context of dementia.

3 Ageing Supernaturally: Dementia in Immortality

In Samuel Taylor Coleridge's poem, *The Rime of the Ancient Mariner* (1817) the unsettling title character imposes his fragmented, repetitive, nonsensical tales on unsuspecting listeners, agonised by an urgency of frantic confession. The poem begins:

> It is an ancient Mariner,
> And he stoppeth one of three.
> 'By thy long beard and glittering eye,
> 'Now wherefore stopp'st thou me?[83]

Those around him are mesmerised, annoyed, even afraid of this man who claims to be caught in a never-ending loop of compulsory storytelling, implying that he exists beyond the span of linearly progressing temporality. Without directly saying that his lifespan is prolonged, he insinuates that his memory significantly deters him from moving forward in time, somewhat like Miss Havisham.

---

[81] Coleridge, *The Rime*, p. 56.   [82] Bryden, *Will I still*, p. 67.   [83] Coleridge, *The Rime*, p. 26.

As explained in the previous section, the ways in which the Mariner returns to the past, gets lost in narrative, struggles to communicate and speaks in fragments – even Coleridge's attempt to interpret for him through the 1817 gloss – resemble dementia experiences and reactions.

One of the defining features of the mariner – in fact, his title feature – is that he's *ancient*, and his age both repels and attracts his young listeners, as shown in illustrations like Figure 2. Any identity beyond this temporal feature is unnecessary, despite the clearly rich and eventful life he recounts in his rime. Age was, and continues to be, a determining factor in the pathologisation of dementia, despite repeated insistence by today's dementia organisations that the disease is not part of 'normal' ageing. Ageing itself leads to an array of conditions not considered to be 'normal' and that necessitate additional diagnosis and treatment, and the position of age as a condition in healthcare remains unclear. This section places the contested relationship between old age and dementia in the context of the Gothic trope of immortality, which separates senescence (the

Figure 2 'I fear thee, ancient Mariner!'
Source: Samuel Taylor Coleridge, *The Rime of the Ancient Mariner*, illustrated by E.H. Wehnert (New York: Appleton & Co., 1857), p. 26.

experience of growing old) and the symptoms of dementia: even characters who claim eternal youth still exhibit moments that resemble dementia symptoms as their nontraditional timelines pose challenges to traditional narrative, communication and memory structures in distressing ways. For a condition often doubly compounded by the stigmas associated with old age and mental illness, this separation makes clear that dementia may be related but not necessarily reliant on other age-related conditions. Margaret Morganroth Gullette defines ageism as 'an ideology based on a master narrative of life-course decline',[84] a *fear* that the life story is coming to an end. But a life could come to an end at any moment, and it is the condition of *prolonged* life that concerns many. Across her oeuvre, disability studies scholar Rosemarie Garland-Thomson warns, 'We will all become disabled *if we live long enough*',[85] to demonstrate the inclusivity of disability and need for widespread advocacy. But, the Gothic reframes this statement as a threat, repeatedly demonstrating the horrors of living 'long enough'.

Despite the cautionary tale of eternal life as torment in the Gothic, the desirability of longevity has historically motivated a wide range of treatments considered, at best, medically unnecessary and, at worst, ridiculously dangerous. Anti-ageing taken to the extreme of eternal life in the Gothic rarely staves off the fears and stigmas associated with growing old, including cognitive alterations and physical alienation. Evading the unrealistic narrative of ageing 'gracefully' results in changes that, if extreme, become symptoms: struggles with communication, identity and memory. But committing to an unrealistic and ageist idea of growing older without alteration is no guarantee that these symptoms can be avoided, either. The Gothic contends that characters who live forever – or at least supernaturally longer than they should – still experience many of the social exclusions anticipated by those who fear old age, let alone dementia. Their refusal to confine themselves to a 'natural' lifespan and a chronological personal history shares characteristics with the defining features of dementia: confusions between past and present, cyclical storytelling, missing or inaccurate memories. As such, Gothic eternal life results in some of the socio-political side effects of dementia as well: disbelief, isolation, and

---

[84] Margaret Morganroth Gullette, 'Against "Aging" – How to Talk about Growing Older', *Theory, Culture & Society* 35:7–8 (2018): 251–270 (p. 252).
[85] Rosemarie Garland-Thomson, 'The Politics of Staring: Visual Rhetorics of Disability in Popular Photography', in Sharon L. Snyder, Brenda Jo Brueggemann, and Rosemarie Garland-Thomson (eds.), *Disability Studies: Enabling the Humanities, Modern Language Association of America* (New York: MLA, 2002), pp. 56–75 (p. 57); Rosemarie Garland-Thomson, *Extraordinary Bodies: Figuring Physical Disability in American Culture and Literature* (New York: Columbia University Press, 2017) p. 14. Emphasis mine.

confinement. Living in altered Gothic timelines through either dementia or immortality becomes a horror in itself.

The equation of dementia with old age negatively impacts depictions of and reactions to both ageing populations and people with dementia, despite many of its symptoms creating an escape from a typical ageing timeline by scrambling memories and disrupting distinctions between past and present. Those with dementia, in other words, may not think of themselves as old, while their caregivers may have trouble seeing past it. The Gothic can further complicate the ageism surrounding this identity-impacting disease by separating age from senescence and mortality. Vampires, deals with the devil, elixirs of eternal life: timelines that move away from mortality strain human bodies and minds with prolonged existence and the experiences and memories that go with it. Living forever is not what these characters expect. I argue that the persistence of symptoms similar to dementia, even in cases of Gothic immortality, challenges the restrictive and socially constructed expectations of ageing 'gracefully' by graphically exposing their potential to intensify aspects of ageing that many fear most. To do this, I consider two texts of Gothic immortality: William Godwin's philosophical Gothic novel, *St. Leon* (1799) and Charles Maturin's labyrinthine classic, *Melmoth the Wanderer* (1820).

3.1 Natural and Supernatural Ageing

In our current cultural moment, fear of old age is partially a fear of dementia, despite medical insistence that age does not necessarily tend that way. The CDC claims that dementia, though 'mostly [affecting] older adults, it is not a part of normal ageing', which is reiterated by the Alzheimer Society of Canada in its advice that memory impairments must be 'so severe that they interfere with your normal daily functions and routines'.[86] And, despite these frequent attempts to isolate dementia from age, a 2019 study of 70,000 people across 155 countries revealed that 'two thirds of people still incorrectly think [Alzheimer's disease] is a normal part of ageing rather than a neurodegenerative disorder',[87] which could lead to confusion, alarm, and increased tensions if ageing becomes mistaken for dementia. No wonder, then, that ageing becomes so feared. Additionally, social pressures to 'age gracefully' and adopt 'anti-ageing' habits put the burden of

---

[86] CDC, 'About Dementia'; Alzheimer Society, 'The Differences between Normal Aging and Dementia', *Alzheimer Society: Canada*, https://alzheimer.ca/en/about-dementia/do-i-have-dementia/differences-between-normal-aging-dementia [last accessed 21 June 2025].

[87] Alzheimer's Disease International, 'World's Largest Dementia Study Reveals Two Thirds of People Still Incorrectly Think Dementia is a Normal Part of Ageing, Rather Than a Medical Condition', *Alzheimer's Disease International*, 1 September 2019, www.alzint.org/news-events/news/worlds-largest-dementia-study-reveals-two-thirds-of-people-still-incorrectly-think-dementia-is-a-normal-part-of-ageing-rather-than-a-medical-condition/ [last accessed 21 June 2025].

Figure 3 A man diagnosed with senile dementia in 1858.
Source: *Medical Times Gazette*, 'Senile Dementia'. Wellcome Collection.

prevention on individuals, overwhelming them with a sea of cultural advice on preventing senescence by maintaining their health through diet, exercise, and good hygiene, all purchased for the right price.[88] Yet, most of this guidance circumvents real health and wellness for mere appearance,[89] an attempt like Miss Havisham's to stop time, but one that is equally doomed to fail.

Dementia has vacillated between age-adjacent and age-dependent since the early nineteenth century, when it was sometimes called 'senile dementia' as shown in Figure 3. Splitting dementia into two different diseases, 'presenile dementia' (for people under sixty) and 'senile dementia' (for people over sixty) in the late nineteenth and early twentieth centuries pathologised age in an official capacity, despite the fact that these distinctions were contested and mostly disregarded, as mentioned in Section 1.[90] When medicine does get involved, arguments for that involvement frame old age as just another disease while arguments against it stem from concerns over interfering with 'natural' life cycles

---

[88] Maginess, 'Introduction', p. 3.   [89] Gullette, 'Against "Aging"', p. 259.
[90] Fletcher 'Pathologisation', p. 14.

and with what it means to be human.[91] Burke points to the assumption that 'good aging is unimpaired, independent, and self-sustaining – in other words, that there is no good aging with dementia'[92] and even those without dementia may encounter system barriers to these 'good ageing' qualities depending on economic and geographic factors. Part of the problem, then, is that both old age and dementia are seen as undesirable, and medicine – from quacks to respected physicians – has peddled advice and treatments to stave off their effects as if they were one and the same.

As discussed in the introduction, dementia has existed within medical discourse since the sixteenth century,[93] but it was only starting to be associated with age in the eighteenth century. Dr John Quincy's 1794 11th edition of *Lexicon Physico-Medicum, or a New Medicinal Dictionary* still defines it simply as 'madness, or a delirium'.[94] As in today's anti-ageing culture, people were expected to adopt habits and regimes to keep themselves healthy for as long as possible. Numerical age held less weight than functionality until the turn of the century when industrialisation triggered a revaluation of the body for its work potential during different times of their day, year, and lifespan, which prompted age to become standardised.[95] Despite dementia's absence from these early discussions of ageing, medical descriptions of senescence bear a resemblance to the disease's symptoms. 'Very old persons', as David Hartley called them in his *Observation on Man* (1749), struggle to access memory or 'the Faculty by which Traces of Sensations and Ideas recur, or are recalled, in the same Order and Proportion, accurately or nearly, as they were once presented', dependent on the 'State of the Brain'.[96] When they recount memories, they merely remember remembering, a memory of a memory, rather than the 'Thing itself', which introduces layers, gaps, and inaccuracies. This 'decay of memory' is just part of their 'dotage', which also includes confusion

---

[91] Eric T. Juengst, 'Anti-Aging Research and the Limits of Medicine', in Stephen G. Post and Robert H. Binstock (eds.), *The Fountain of Youth: Cultural, Scientific, and Ethical Perspectives on a Biomedical Goal* (Oxford: Oxford University Press, 2004), pp. 321–339 (p. 326).

[92] Lucy Burke, 'Spectres of Unproductive Life', in Katie Aubrecht, Christine Kelly, and Carla Rice (eds.), *The Aging-Disability Nexus* (Toronto: UBC Press, 2020), pp. 35–50 (p. 36).

[93] *Oxford English Dictionary*, 'dementia (n.)', March 2025, https://doi.org/10.1093/OED/7488111706.

[94] Originally published in 1717. The entry for 'Dementia' is just above the entry for 'Demonia: melancholy from the influence of evil spirits'. Quincy, *Lexicon Physico-Medicum*, p. 265.

[95] Jacob Jewusiak, *Aging, Duration, and the English Novel: Growing Old from Dickens to Woolf* (Cambridge: Cambridge University Press, 2019), pp. 5–6; Patrick Fox, 'From Senility to Alzheimer's Disease: The Rise of the Alzheimer's Disease Movement', *The Milbank Quarterly* 67:1 (1989): 58–102 (p. 61); Susanna R. Ottaway, *The Decline of Life: Old Age in Eighteenth-Century England* (Cambridge: Cambridge University Press, 2004), pp. 7–8, 44.

[96] David Hartley, *Observations on Man: His Frame, His Duty, and His Expectations*, Vol. 1 (Cambridge: Cambridge University Press, 2013), pp. 268–415 (p. 374).

about the present as their brains languish and their bones waste.[97] Pathologisation of weakness, memory loss, and confusion such as this might be so distressing that, as Ella Sbaraini has shown, incidents of suicide amongst older people were particularly high in the eighteenth century, caused by a combination of economic and social factors: losing the ability to provide for themselves, alongside increased isolation and lessening health and mental faculties made death seem desirable. In the age of rising industrialisation, a nonproductive body is seen as a burden.[98]

The idea that dementia, senescence in general, and even death might be negotiable was not restricted to medical debate. In *Enquiry Concerning Political Justice, and Its Influences on General Virtue and Happiness* (1793), William Godwin claims that freedom and morality – not medicine – are the keys to immortality. Negative habits and moods are largely responsible for physical and mental deterioration, just as positive outlooks can impact medical outcomes. 'Mature man' gets old because he 'desists from youthful habits. He assumes an air of dignity, incompatible with the lightness of childish fallies', and 'every time that our mind becomes morbid, vacant and melancholy, our eternal frame falls into disorder', and he further blames mental states like anxiety, discontent, rage, revenge, and despair for '[corroding] the frame, and hourly [consigning] their miserable victims to an untimely grave'.[99] No wonder Gothic characters so desperately seek eternal youth, though it does little to lessen these toxic emotions. Because Godwin implies individual control over the ageing process, Andrea Charise remarks that he posits senescence as a state rather than a stage of the human lifespan, also pointing to Godwin's Gothic novel, *St. Leon* as a 'significant revision' of Godwin's ideas about immortality, now portraying it as anything but desirable.[100]

In rethinking age as a state rather than a stage, Charise and Godwin remove senescence from a temporal framework, opening up possibilities for it to occur at any time and repeatedly as a matter of will and 'chearfulness'.[101] Both St. Leon and Melmoth, the title characters of Godwin and Maturin's novels whose lifespans have been supernaturally altered, do experience moments of senescence, thereby dispelling the expectation that eternal life precludes moments of pain, ageing, and potentially dementia. They do so outside typical timelines, however,

---

[97] Hartley, *Observations*, pp. 380, 392–393.

[98] Ella Sbaraini, 'The Ageing Body, Memory-Loss and Suicide in Georgian England', *Social History of Medicine* 35:1 (2021): 170–194.

[99] William Godwin, *Enquiry Concerning Political Justice, and its Influences on General Virtue and Happiness* (London: G.G.J. and J. Robinson, 1793), pp. 522–523.

[100] Andrea Charise, '"The Tyranny of Age": Godwin's *St. Leon* and the Nineteenth-Century Longevity Narrative', *ELH* 79:4 (Winter 2012): 905–933 (p. 907).

[101] Godwin, *Enquiry*, p. 522.

St. Leon ageing in stages that are both early and reversible and Melmoth ageing rapidly in his last moments of life. In *Melmoth the Wanderer*, Melmoth makes a deal with the devil for an extended lifespan of 150 years, freeing him from the conventions of both time and space while he searches for someone to replace him, starting the 150 years anew. He seeks out many desperate characters, appearing to their amazement 'without a hair on his head changed, or a muscle in his frame contracted', but none will make the trade.[102] Meanwhile, during moments when he is tempted by the mortal world, he feels a ghostly internal decay of his immortal body and doomed soul, 'gnawings of the worm that never dies', 'scorchings of the fire that is never to be quenched', and the 'fire that was consuming his vitals'.[103] On the last night of his life, Melmoth ages quickly and dramatically, a transformation that is described as horrific by onlookers: 'the lines of extreme age were visible in every feature. His hairs were as white as snow, his mouth had fallen in, the muscles of his face were relaxed and withered – he was the very image of hoary decrepit debility', and this senescence is not just a scary skin-deep development. Melmoth 'started' at the response, replying, 'You see what I feel.'[104] His death follows soon after.

Similarly, St. Leon, after gambling away all his wealth and forcing his family into poverty, assists a stranger who shares with him the 'art of multiplying gold and the power of living forever'.[105] As a result, he claims superhuman health in his first-person narrative, thinking himself 'invulnerable to disease. Every sun that rises, finds the circulation of my frame in the most perfect order. Decreptitude can never approach me', while celebrating 'perpetual vigour, perpetual activity, perpetual youth' free from any signs of ageing or decay as he is 'triumphant over fate and time!'[106] He spends most of this time and the novel in one dungeon or prison after another, however, as his sudden wealth and lack of visible ageing prevent him from ever integrating back into the society he left long ago. Even as ageing is pathologised, not ageing is demonised, leaving no acceptable alternatives, even in the Gothic. During an episode when he does not 'triumph' over time, St. Leon prematurely ages even beyond his natural years after spending twelve years in a Spanish Inquisition cell, claiming to look eighty when he is only fifty-four. Upon seeing his reflection after escaping, he mentions the same white hair and lined face that Melmoth experiences but also that his mind 'had subsided into childishness' and 'been as much cribbed and immured as my body. I was the mere shadow of a man, of no more power and worth than that which a magic lantern produces upon a wall'.[107] Not only does

---

[102] Maturin, *Melmoth*, p. 27.   [103] Maturin, *Melmoth*, p. 299.   [104] Maturin, *Melmoth*, p. 540.
[105] William Godwin, *St. Leon*, edited by William D. Brewer (Peterborough: Broadview Press, 2006), p. 185.
[106] Godwin, *St. Leon*, pp. 53, 67.   [107] Godwin, *St. Leon*, p. 341.

his body feel weak and aged, his mind alters, and he notes the social dismissal of senescence as a physical sensation. Here we see the dangerous attitudes towards age that Sabaraini describes, and, after he takes the elixir of life to return himself to his twenties, he distances himself from the experience by remarking of *other* older people, 'with what a melancholy sensation does the old man survey his decaying limbs! To me, he cries, there is no second morning, and no returning spring ... the memory answers no other end than to torment and upbraid me', using Gothic language to illustrate the fears of experiencing an ageing body, mind, and socio-political status.[108] According to St. Leon, memory (for the 'old man', not himself) can only bring pain. However, St. Leon doth protest too much here, his own experience of senescence proving even more terrifying for its inadherence to a normative timeline, and his memories are anything but comforting. Despite their claims of independence from the diminishing, humiliating, and even dehumanising impacts of ageing, both Melmoth and St. Leon experience symptoms referenced in historical medical texts and in today's cultural perceptions that inconsistently connect dementia to age. Despite their hyper-healthy youth, they experience moments of madness, disorientation, miscommunication, and forgetfulness in concentrated forms.

3.2 Hyper-Healthy: Dementia among the Immortals

Gothic characters with supernaturally expanded lifespans, then, report moments of confusion, memory loss and troubled identity similar to symptoms associated with dementia. Without diagnosing them with this cognitive illness, however, we can at least say they are not experiencing what might be seen as 'healthy' or 'graceful' ageing in any time period. And, despite their supposed freedom from senescence, they occasionally form new disturbing links between their age and their symptoms. Each symptom discussed in this section arises because of the combination of supernatural longevity and excess health, starting with identity changes. Readers will expect Gothic characters to shift their identity throughout a text, as discussed in previous sections. St. Leon self-reports personality changes as if he were talking about characters separate from himself, occasionally resorting to third-person point of view. An unreliable husband and father who regularly falls into fits of ineptitude while failing to protect his family, he claims to do so because he loves them. Yet, once he takes the elixir, he reports 'my domestic character was ... wholly destroyed' and 'If I still loved my wife and children, it was the love of habit rather than sympathy', reporting a 'deadness of heart' shortly after beginning immortality.[109] St. Leon and Melmoth both eventually fall into the role of passive observer for parts of

---

[108] Godwin, *St. Leon*, p. 345.   [109] Godwin, *St. Leon*, pp. 192, 229, 189.

their expanded lifespan as they grapple with their inability to participate, change, and grow at the pace of those around them. As described by one witness, Melmoth appears at a wedding where no one knows him and he merely smiles vacantly as if lost or deluded, speaking to no one. Melmoth's role of observer has purpose: to collect candidates who become so desperate they would give up their souls. Active participation would make him too known, too feared, something St. Leon learns the hard way. He develops paranoia and 'imaginary plots and dangers' that cause him to act erratically in front of people already suspicious of his powers. Each time St. Leon moves to escape an angry mob, he must reinvent himself anew while maintaining protective isolation until he 'more resembled a piece of furniture endowed with the faculty of noting the sensations of those around me, than the member of any human society'.[110] Hating his immortality, St. Leon describes, 'From this hour I had no passions, no interests, no affections', which, according to Godwin's *Enquiry*, should rapidly result in senescence. Instead, it partially drives other forms of psychological decline from which his eternal youth fails to shield him. Both Melmoth and St. Leon also shift identities in response to increasing isolation, a situation common for people with dementia.

St. Leon's first-person tale provides intimate access to his Gothic narrative tendencies, exposing shifts in identity, time and memory that the character may not even realise. Getting lost in navigating both past and present as a result of confusion and memory loss is a symptom mentioned in both historical texts and current literature on dementia. Kruger describes it as 'the inability to construct stories or to be assimilated by anyone else into a coherent narrative view of life', and St. Leon's narrative exposes his struggles with storytelling, calling into question his own self-awareness.[111] For one, his introduction to his story clearly contradicts what the tale actually includes. He declares, 'Everything that I see almost, I can without difficulty make my own . . . I can command, to an extent almost inconceivable, the passions of men. What heart can withstand the assault of princely magnificence? What man is inaccessible to a bribe?' Apparently, all hearts and all men. Every attempt to bribe someone or impress them with wealth spectacularly *fails* in this novel, leaving St. Leon immortally powerless to support these claims with his experiences.[112] He frequently steps out of the narrative to mix tenses in commentary on his own writing process, seeming to exist simultaneously in 'dwelling' and 'anticipating' while speaking to characters long gone as if they were present before him. He calls attention to gaps in his narrative, mentioning unrelated incidents only to announce he is passing

---

[110] Godwin, *St. Leon*, p. 357.   [111] Kruger, 'The "Terrifying Question Mark"', p. 109.
[112] Godwin, *St. Leon*, p. 53.

over them, though these gaps are not as visually noticeable as those found in *Melmoth the Wanderer* discussed in Section 2.[113]

Melmoth only occasionally speaks in first-person in a novel with excessively layered narrative frames. Instead, a range of found documents and scraps of story create gaps that involve participants beyond the immortal, building a community of Melmoth witnesses even if he is excluded from accessing it directly. St. Leon's gaps are of his own making, which he seemingly stumbles into by surprise as he recounts his tale from his particularly erratic memory. Further, it is unclear whether St. Leon expects his narrative to have an audience or whether it is simply an extended conversation with himself. On one hand, he resigns, 'It is no matter that these pages shall never be surveyed by other eyes than mine', but then also directly addresses a reader when he challenges, 'I have no power to talk of the situation in which I was now placed, and the reader must therefore explain it for himself, – if he can.'[114] He even reacts defensively as if an invented audience had demanded to know the science behind his powers, snapping, 'Such readers I have only to remind, that the pivot upon which the history I am composing turns, is a mystery. If they will not accept of my communication upon my own terms, they must lay aside my book', emotionally responding to imaginary demands only he can hear.[115] Along with an audience, he also invents third-person commentators and what they say about him: 'I have no ties to existence. St. Leon has no wife; St. Leon has no child; he has neither connection nor friend in the world.'[116] Finally, even when immortal characters produce coherent communication, they face a familiar and daunting challenge familiar to people with dementia: that of not being believed. Both the stranger who gives St. Leon the elixir and Melmoth discredit themselves by talking about people and events that existed too far in the past for them to have known them personally, convincing listeners that their words are mere delusion.

Uncertainty about audience, time, and identity are compounded by the confusion of both memory loss and memory overwhelm as well as St. Leon's references to his 'infant mind'.[117] In true Gothic fashion, St. Leon is clearly haunted by both the memories of his neglected and lost family and his fears that he fabricated their existence, wondering, 'Were there really such persons? Where are they dispersed? ... I see nothing around me but speechless walls, or human faces that say as little to my heart as the walls themselves.'[118] He continually interrupts his narrative to flee from these memories and the people in them, which he finds unmanageable and painful, sometimes speaking to them as if they are present. At other moments, they clog the narrative with senseless

---

[113] Godwin, *St. Leon*, p. 171.   [114] Godwin, *St. Leon*, pp. 186, 297.
[115] Godwin, *St. Leon*, p. 230.   [116] Godwin, *St. Leon*, p. 396.
[117] Godwin, *St. Leon*, pp. 206, 210, 341.   [118] Godwin, *St. Leon*, p. 164.

fragments, just as they did for the stranger in *St. Leon* close to his end, when he repeated 'Clara! – Henry! – a friend! a friend! – and then he would groan as if his heart were bursting', foreshadowing St. Leon's reciprocal experience of rolling his eyes, biting his tongue and muttering, 'My son! my son! – wealth! wealth! – my wife! – my son!'[119] Though the reader understands St. Leon's references here because they have been privy to his entire narrative, those around him cannot interpret this outburst, and there are no further clues to the stranger's meaning. When St. Leon gets to the end of his narrative, he starts repeating details about his son he has already shared, starting to cycle back to previous incidents as if he does not know what else to do. His repetition harkens back to the Ancient Mariner as he seems in danger of compulsively restarting parts of his tale anew. When time is no longer relevant, those with expanded lifespans have no incentive to maintain a linear chronology of their lives. The order, gaps, and repetitions – all features shared with symptoms of dementia – become as meaningless as distinctions between past, present, and future.

3.3 Limits of the Human: Body and Mind

Despite their quests for immortality, Gothic characters with supernaturally altered lifespans sooner or later idolise death as a defining factor that they think makes them human. St. Leon is unlike Melmoth in that he made no deal with the devil, but he feels cursed all the same. St. Leon later remarks that he should have taken the stranger's eagerness to die more seriously. Not unlike older people in the eighteenth century who chose suicide to escape the isolation, guilt and burden of growing dependency, St. Leon feels as if he has already committed the deed, remarking, 'I became prematurely dead to my country and my race, because I was destined never to die!'[120] The unsettling wish for death has an even more unsettling place within the context of dementia. As Christ soberly reminds us, 'Narrations with dementia become end-of-life narrations.'[121] It is not uncommon to hear family and friends express relief upon dementia ending in death because they 'lost' that person or that person 'died' long ago, the disease having altered them to such an extent. St. Leon and Melmoth experience this same metaphorical death without the actual end, at least not for St. Leon. But, in the Gothic, death is rarely the end of anyone's narrative, whether they continue to haunt in memory alone or in more physical forms. Despite his hyper-health, Melmoth is speculated to be dead when he tells stories involving people from long ago, and even the Ancient Mariner, whose mortality is unknown, is suspected to be dead by his listener, though he assures

---

[119] Godwin, *St. Leon*, pp. 169, 213.   [120] Godwin, *St. Leon*, p. 303.
[121] Christ, *Fictions of Dementia*, p. 26.

him, 'This body dropt not down.'[122] Nonetheless, both the Mariner and Melmoth's listeners fear them, their immortality excluding them from human timelines as another form of death. Importantly, however, as readers we know that, despite their struggles with communication, memory confusion, and human connection, Melmoth and St Leon still have valuable narratives that are accessible in the context of Gothic storytelling.

Prior to his sudden death and during his accelerated ageing, Melmoth makes a point of insisting, 'my existence is still human' to justify his need for rest, care, even compassion. It is not surprising that he needs to clarify his humanity, having 'obtained from the enemy of souls a range of existence beyond the period allotted to mortality – a power to pass over space without disturbance or delay', regardless of physical obstruction.[123] Unrestricted by normative senses of time and space, along with incoherent communication and unstable identities, Melmoth and St. Leon face dehumanisation in their hyper-healthy states, just as people with dementia encounter dehumanisation for similar misunderstandings of time and space in pathologised ageing states. In short, extreme health does not prevent the exclusion and dismissal that are feared results of ageing, despite the supposed desirability of eternal youth. St. Leon expresses dismay at the 'immeasurable distance that was put between me and the rest of my species. I found myself alone in the world', referring to 'the gulf that cut me off from everything that deserves the name of human'.[124] In the next two sections, I will explore further the tendency to dehumanise people diagnosed with dementia as negligible, unbelievable, even frightening for their struggles to communicate, understand, and care for themselves. But here, Melmoth and St. Leon are hardly considered negligible because of apparent age, implying that narrative, identity and communication, even for those who are superior in physical health, still result in dismissal and exclusion. Further, just as Melmoth requires care and compassion in his last moments, St. Leon seeks out the care of his family. Near the end of his narrative, he finds his son, Charles, but in this version of himself St. Leon is a decade younger than him and, thereby, looks to him for guidance and protection as a stranger in need. The parent has become the child, a familiar but problematic dementia narrative of role reversal and age regression that reduces agency while increasing dependence. Despite St. Leon's Gothic cycle of supernatural hyper-health, the mental and psychological impact of living forever produces many of the cognitive behaviours of both those with dementia and historical pathologies of senescence, suggesting that supernatural lifespans in Gothic timelines do not lead to hopeful futures.

---

[122] Coleridge, *The Rime*, pp. 46–47.   [123] Maturin, *Melmoth*, p. 538.
[124] Godwin, *St. Leon*, p. 297.

4 Lost Selves: The Demon in Dementia

The temptation of eternal youth remains strong in the twenty-first century as youthful characters fear growing old and ageing characters mourn the loss of their younger years. At the end of the film *The Manor* (Axelle Carolyn, 2021), the ease with which the newly septuagenarian protagonist, Judith, chooses a return to youth by becoming a parasitic witch is jarring. Just moments earlier, she had been a victim of such witches herself, and the film directs sympathy towards their victims. But, fear is a powerful motivator, and they are all victims of the larger threat of growing older in a culture that values youth. Unlike the literary texts previously discussed, the films included in this section feature characters explicitly diagnosed with or noticeably developing symptoms of dementia. As such, they bear additional responsibility for the challenging task of depicting this familiar and feared disease in ways that represent both the illness experiences of those close to dementia *and* the wider cultural anxieties surrounding it. The results heavily favour the latter. Like most horror films that engage with the topics of physical and mental illness and disability, they fall under scrutiny for damaging contributions to negative perceptions of dementia that could hinder seeking out or offering care. Despite extensive research investments, the lack of practical action to prevent or cure dementia (so far) makes it a fear amplified by the little that can be done to prepare.

Horror and its use of Gothic narrative conventions – atemporal timelines, nonnormative narrative structures and unstable identities – make it a fitting mode for navigating an illness that, despite the best efforts of medical staff, activists, and scholars, *is* frightening. The history of medicine includes a long legacy of patient fear, ranging from fear of contracting disease to fear of diagnosis and the resulting treatment, as well as fear of stigma within and without medical spaces. Goldman goes so far as to claim that 'the term "dementia" has been Gothicized ... [evoking] the "dreadful" image of an elderly individual suffering'.[125] Read another way, the Gothic provides a shared language and frame of reference to express dread that may already exist. To depict the dementia experience without fear may comfort some viewers, but it could also be seen as disingenuous and alienating, as discussed in the introduction. Cultural anxiety about dementia and growing old in general is undeniable, and the Gothic and horror are spaces to put those toxic emotions, where they can be felt and examined. Leaning into the aspects of dementia that scare us, even in gruesome ways, can acknowledge those apprehensions and provide insights into why those emotions occur.

---

[125] Goldman, *Forgotten*, p. 64.

Horror may be well situated to represent dementia, but that does not mean it always handles this responsibility wisely or ethically. This section and the next will deconstruct two different approaches to the fear inherent in the dementia experience. For the films discussed in Section 5, fear is rooted in the disease itself, the supernatural merely making it more visible. But the films discussed in Section 4 – *The Manor, The Taking of Deborah Logan* (Adam Robitel, 2014), and *Old people* (Andy Fetscher, 2022) – rely explicitly on the supernatural (demonic possession, witches, zombies) to tease but ultimately circumvent direct engagement with dementia as the true source of fear. For these films, the Gothic supernatural triggers suspicions of people with dementia but ultimately lessens their monstrosity by proving to be a much more potent threat. The diversion of supernatural entities in these films, then, neglects an opportunity to recognise dementia as a worthy Gothic and horror theme on its own and demonstrates how a dementia diagnosis can dominate narratives even amidst other explanations. Each film punishes dismissal of older people with far worse Gothic horrors perpetuated by reducing individuals to their disease. Drawing on the Gothic's ability to blur the lines between science and the supernatural and its willingness to witness disturbing experiences, these films unsettle notions of human control to champion those assumed to be powerless. They subvert dementia symptoms into Gothic instruments of monstrosity.

4.1 Dementia in Horror

Horror films aside, identity alterations in people with dementia can make them seem unlike themselves to the point that they may appear to act like strangers. Their behaviour may seem automatic rather than self-aware, and their moods may swing drastically from one moment to the next, remembering and then not remembering, recognising and then not recognising. It should be little surprise that, amidst the emotions of sadness, anger, and loss, the cruel metaphors of monstrosity, possession, and zombies practically write themselves. A familiar body inhabited by a strange spirit may be the closest frame of reference for family and friends, even people with dementia themselves, to understand this distressing experience. Does this easily available cultural reference help or hinder real responses to dementia? In *The Manor*, Judith chooses to institutionalise herself to prevent her declining health from becoming a burden to her family, a noble but perhaps unnecessary sacrifice to make while she is cognitively and physically able. The contrast between herself and the others in the Manor is undeniable, and the audience shares her growing fear that she may become like them by being there. Being around ageing bodies and minds does not increase her sympathy for them; it increases her defensiveness and (she thinks) instigates her own decline into mental and physical fragility.

Horror, then, tends to dehumanise older people and older women in particular, which serves to increase rather than close the distance between viewers and people with dementia, though the study cited in the introduction suggests effects are more nuanced than this. To see someone as less than human suggests that there's no need to treat them as human, impacting human rights and basic dignity. Worse, it can infer that acting against people with dementia in some way protects everyone else. Gothic and horror metaphors like the zombie or demonic possession are tempting: people with dementia may be seen to shuffle slowly, speak incoherently, exhibit disorientation, and lose control over their bodies. Agnieszka Kotwasińska points to dementia's 'symptoms of bodily and mental disintegration (such as short-term memory loss, communication difficulties, disorientation, withdrawal from society, loss of bodily functions, weakened immunological system)', which it shares with demonic possession.[126] When confronted with someone who has been possessed or bitten by a zombie, the standard mantra is 'it's not the person you know', or 'the person you knew is gone', to justify killing them. These comparisons impact not just family members and caregivers for people with dementia but also people who may face this diagnosis in the future. I have been disturbed to hear people say they would 'rather be dead than have dementia' or than 'become a burden on their family', just as characters in zombie moves make pacts to end their lives if they are bitten.[127] As Susan M. Buhuniak writes, 'Although a terminal disease can invoke a dread of death, it is not so much death by AD [Alzheimer's disease] that terrifies but the proposition that patients will be dehumanised through social construction as the "living dead"'.[128] Fears of dehumanisation in vulnerable medical spaces and care homes already abound. This inspired early dementia studies work advocating for people with dementia to be treated like people, which will be discussed more in Section 5.

Horror films do not just participate in negative associations that already exist; they also exaggerate them to excess, disconnecting them from the status of realistic representation. At the same time, these creative excesses may achieve what Sally Chivers notes is missing from most cinematic depictions of ageing characters: 'the plots that concern aging to date generally do not celebrate its

---

[126] Agnieszka Kotwasińska, 'Un/re/production of Old Age in The Taking of Deborah Logan', *Somatechnics* 8.2 (2018): 178–194 (pp. 183–184).

[127] Buhuniak claims that 'scholars also apparently feel free to apply the living dead metaphor when they study people with AD [Alzheimer's Disease]'. The comparison is pervasive. Susan M. Buhuniak, 'The Living Dead? The Construction of People with Alzheimer's Disease as Zombies', *Ageing & Society* 31 (2011): 70–92 (p. 79).

[128] Buhuniak, *The Living Dead*, p. 77.

possibilities but rather ... revel in its disadvantages'.[129] They are deficit-based narratives. While horror does revel in the disadvantages, particularly those of a graphic nature, its ability to consider possibilities is underappreciated as it uses the supernatural to grant characters with dementia extraordinary power, for good or evil. Unlike genres that draw on sentimentalism, horror characters with dementia tend to fight back. In their study of ageing and horror, Cynthia J. Miller and A. Bowdoin Van Riper point out that, 'as narratives of "old and in the way" are increasingly questioned, the tension between ability and disability in the elderly has also begun to receive more nuanced and focused consideration', framing the reversed power dynamics of horror as potential triumph.[130] Horror vacillates between the extremes of helplessness and power, subverting the simplicity of metaphors, even ones for which it may be responsible. The films discussed in this section portray people with dementia as monstrous but reveal that the direct cause of their symptoms is supernatural rather than medical, meaning they *are* in fact monstrous, but not because they have dementia. Rather pathologisation *of* dementia has a role in making these monsters.

4.2 Medicine or Magic: Interpreting Dementia Symptoms

In *The Taking of Deborah Logan (Deborah Logan)*, dementia is used as an entry into demonic possession, calling attention to its symptoms and their impact as resembling dementia symptoms until it surpasses them. Deborah and her daughter Sarah are the subject of a student medical documentary created by Mia and her crew that will offer insights into Alzheimer's disease (see Figure 4). Opinionated, independent, and clearly used to managing her own home, Deborah exhibits classic symptoms of dementia: confusion, mood swings, memory loss, difficulty finding words, forgetfulness, disorientation, and strange behaviours especially at night. At other times, she is intelligent, coherent, and dignified, still in the beginning stages the disease. Increased episodes of violence towards herself and others give way to more unusual symptoms, such as speaking foreign languages she does not know and vomiting earthworms. Dementia becomes an excuse to dismiss what is really happening to Deborah. While doctors persist in attempting to explain these symptoms within medical contexts, their interpretations continually fail, and it is only when Sarah looks beyond dementia that she can see other possibilities. While everyone is focused on the 'problem' of Deborah's progressing dementia symptoms, she has become possessed by the

---

[129] Sally Chivers, *The Silvering Screen: Old Age and Disability in Cinema* (Toronto: University of Toronto Press, 2011), p. xx.

[130] Cynthia J. Miller and A. Bowdoin Van Riper, 'Introduction', in Cynthia J. Miller and A. Bowdoin Van Riper (eds.), *Elder Horror: Essays on Film's Frightening Images of Aging* (Jefferson: McFarland, 2019), pp. 1–9 (p. 3).

Figure 4 Deborah is under constant surveillance in her home and in the hospital.
Source: *The Taking of Deborah Logan*, directed by Adam Robitel (Guerin-Adler-Scott Pictures, 2014).

evil spirit of a child serial killer she killed long ago to protect young Sarah. In this case, the horror trope of demonic possession exposes the frightening potential for interpretive failure in medical diagnosis that neglects patient narrative.

Scholarship on *Deborah Logan* untangles the complex relationship between age and gender in the context of social status, body image, and motherhood.[131] Scholars have argued that the film both exposes and subverts lost social relevance and sex status, and, because most work on this film references gender and age in the context of Barbara Creed's concept of the 'Monstrous-Feminine', I will not repeat similar readings here.[132] Without disagreeing with arguments like Maddie McGillvrey's that Deborah is 'represented as a monster simply because she is old and riddled with disease', my parallel argument addresses

---

[131] See Dawn Keetley, 'The Shock of Aging (Women) in Horror Film', in Cynthia J. Miller and A. Bowdoin Van Riper (eds.), *Elder Horror: Essays on Film's Frightening Images of Aging* (Jefferson: McFarland, 2019), pp. 58–69; Morgan Batch and Mark David Ryan, 'Dementia and Contemporary Horror Movies: Gendered Ageing and the Haunted Home', *New Review of Film and Television Studies* 22.3 (2024): 760–780.

[132] See Marta Miquel-Baldellou, 'From the Female Grotesque to the Crone: Beware of the Older Woman in *The Taking of Deborah Logan* (2014)', in Noelia Gregorio-Fernández and Carmen M. Méndez-García (eds.), *Culture Wars and Horror Movies: Gender Debates in Post-2010's US Horror Cinema* (New York: Palgrave Macmillan, 2024), pp. 183–203; Maddie McGillvrey, '"To Grandmother's House We Go": Documenting the Horror of the Aging Woman in Found Footage Films', in Cynthia J. Miller and A. Bowdoin Van Riper (eds.), *Elder Horror: Essays on Film's Frightening Images of Aging* (Jefferson: McFarland, 2019), pp. 70–80; and Kotwasińska, 'Un/re/production'.

misinterpretations of dementia in the film and what monsters they ultimately allow to thrive. Defining Deborah as monstrous because of her age and disease and nothing else prevents other defining aspects of her life from being seen. The power of this defining medical monstrosity persuades characters in all three films to take drastic measures offered by Gothic monstrosity: to become one type of monster to avoid continuing on as another.

Both early dementia studies and disability studies have approached medicine's pathologisation of nonnormative forms of embodiment with uneasy scepticism. James Rupert Fletcher goes so far as to say that 'Early dementia studies was anti-medicine', because medicine 'legitimised undue institutional control over the people diagnosed while simultaneously delegitimizing those people by attributing their experiences and behaviours to a disease'.[133] In fact, Joanna Braun reads the resistance to medical cure within possession narratives as a similar resistance to the problematic medical model of disability.[134] Even the health or medical humanities cautions against the neglect of human complexity over objective medical categories in subfields like narrative medicine that emphasise listening to and reading patients as stories. At the same time, dementia, like the Gothic itself, defies easy classification, let alone what actions should be taken in response, if any. As Linn J. Sandberg and Richard Ward describe, 'The canons of disability studies and social gerontology ... have been built largely through exclusion of dementia. There remains an unspoken anxiety that opening up to dementia might risk "re-medicalising" the hard-fought territory of sociological understandings of later life built up through discourses of successful and positive ageing.'[135] The fact is, despite the risk of dehumanisation, medical care and support is often vital for people with dementia, despites its socio-political dangers.

As in most possession narratives, the medical narratives in *Deborah Logan* repeatedly fail as they attempt to explain Deborah's behaviours. Unstable identities are accentuated in the context of the found footage tradition, in which performativity is laid bare and calls every behaviour into question. While the realism implied by continuous filming may seem to remove opportunities for performance, we see characters repeatedly wondering how they should act, how they should 'be' to fit into the medical narrative the students intend to capture. This multi-layered reality makes the medical narrative seem even more contrived and unreliable. When they bring Deborah into the hospital, doctors tell Sarah that the disease has advanced to the middle stages, despite

---

[133] Fletcher, *The Biopolitics*, p. 30.
[134] Joanna Braun, *Performing Hysteria: Images and Imaginations of Hysteria* (Leuven: Leuven University Press, 2020), pp. 223–224.
[135] Sandberg and Ward, 'Introduction', p. 2.

having previously described a timeline of at least three years to reach that point. We see the same unreliability of medical narrative in *The Manor*, not because it fails but because it lies. From its position beyond lay understanding – a position that makes science easily interchangeable with the supernatural in classic Gothic texts – medical authorities fabricate data that is used to diagnose and consequently discredit Judith, just as she is beginning to report feeling unsafe in the facility. This is an abrupt shift from her arrival, feeling confident in her proactive decision to enter the nursing home while still independent and feeling good: 'my prognosis isn't good. My symptoms are under control for now, but who knows how long that will last. Whatever's coming next, whenever, however I end up diminished, I don't want my family to see me like that', she says. What diminishes her, however, is the witchcraft facilitated by the staff rather than the feared senescence of age and dementia.[136] That Judith then anticipates worsening dementia symptoms is also an act of self-sabotage, reinforcing a speculative medical narrative of deficit and doubting her future self as a reliable narrator in advance of her decline. In lieu of this diagnosis, she is not even worthy of inclusion in discussions about her treatment, to which only her daughter is now privy, insisting, 'We're all trying to look after you, I promise'. Similarly, in *Deborah Logan*, even the priest Sarah asks to perform an exorcism privileges the unconvincing medical narrative, insisting that she 'needs to accept this'. Once a dementia diagnosis is established, it changes one's relationship with their own narrative and how it will be received, subsuming all other meanings.

In putting medical narratives alongside demonic possession, *Deborah Logan* reveals an uneasy parallel between healthcare and supernatural ritual, joining a long history of possession films in which medicine cannot cope with the causes and symptoms outside their restricted, rational purview. We see the same thing in *The Exorcist* and its sequels, many of which include painful inconclusive hospital scenes. The Gothic takes advantage of what Elana Commisso calls 'medical indeterminacy', the vast inconsistencies and unknowns about dementia (and indeed most cognitive and mental illnesses) that can prevent early and accurate medical certainty and commitment.[137] Sarah's investigation of video recordings of Deborah's incomprehensible speech, hunt for clues around the house, and research in archives to understand Deborah's experiences mimic the less successful exploratory tests and surveillance of the hospital. Even the

---

[136] Incidentally, one of the witches is played by Jill Larson, who also plays Deborah Logan.

[137] Elana Commisso, 'The Zero-Degree of Dementia: Thinking the Gap between Subject and Substance', in Aagje Swinnen and Mark Schweda (eds.), *Popularizing Dementia: Public Expressions and Representations of Forgetfulness* (New York: Columbia University Press, 2016), pp. 377–401(p. 377).

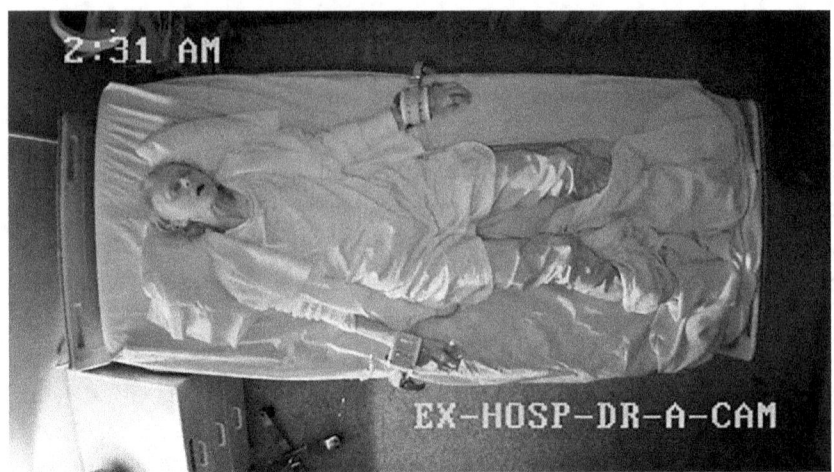

Figure 5 Deborah is restrained in the hospital.
Source: *The Taking of Deborah Logan*, directed by Adam Robitel (Guerin-Adler-Scott Pictures, 2014).

demonic use of snakes subverts the purity of the medical caduceus. While the doctors seem knowledgeable and kind, their management of Deborah's symptoms fail because their fixation on first dementia, then schizophrenia, prevents them from considering other possibilities. The staff loses control over Deborah with each test and, despite her obvious distress, they physically restrain her and stop communicating with her, again mimicking common scenes in possession films (see Figure 5).

Despite the seeming antiquation of this treatment, these scenes are not necessarily the Gothic stepping in and regressing the hospital back through medical history, despite its tendency to do so. Herein lies the source of our greatest fears. The World Health Organization claims that in the twenty-first century, 'people living with dementia are frequently denied the basic rights and freedoms available to others. In many countries, physical and chemical restraints are used extensively ... even when regulations are in place to uphold the rights of people to freedom and choice'.[138] We do see moments of real tenderness between Sarah and Deborah, as seen in Figure 6, but Sarah's overriding feelings of frustration and depression make those moments rare and fleeting. The shift from talking to Deborah when she's at home to talking about her during these hospital scenes are even more notable once Sarah sees Deborah's possession over her dementia. Conversations with and about her

---

[138] WHO, 'Dementia', *World Health Organization*, 31 March 2025, www.who.int/news-room/fact-sheets/detail/dementia[last accessed 22 June 2025].

Figure 6 Mother and daughter try to stay positive for the camera.
Source: *The Taking of Deborah Logan*, directed by Adam Robitel (Guerin-Adler-Scott Pictures, 2014).

mother with dementia are cruelly patronising, emphasising her lost abilities; conversations with and about her mother possessed by a serial killer insist on her power and humanity, calling on her to 'fight him, Ma!' If, as Buhuniak accuses, the biomedical model 'reinforces the notion of the patient with [Alzheimer's disease] as a non-person', the Gothic's revelation that something more supernatural and uncanny is at work ironically *re*humanises Deborah.[139] Demonic possession is read as separate from her rather than inherent, prompting less judgement despite the obvious association with monstrosity enhanced by her gruesome physical transformations.

4.3 The Horror of Not Being Believed

One of the Gothic's hallmarks is that, as David Punter writes, 'it deals with those moments when we find it impossible, with any degree of hope, for our "case to be put"'.[140] In other words, the Gothic navigates the horror of not being believed, whether it be at the hands of institutional gaslighting, local discrediting, or systemic irrelevance. In dementia, this lost believability is compounded by the symptom of communication challenges such that individuals may not be cognitively able to tell their stories in a conventional manner or at all. This partially inspires the attitude that they have reverted to being children. Valerie Keller reminds us that, even though their dependency may resemble that of children, they do not think of themselves that way and 'can look back on a rather long life' that includes systemic

---

[139] Buhuniak, 'The Living Dead', p. 74.
[140] David Punter, *Gothic Pathologies: The Text, the Body and the Law* (New York: St. Martin's Press, 1998), p. 5.

and individual traumas as well as successes and joys.[141] In the Manor, Judith curses when she is upset, and the staff react as if she were a naughty child, setting her up to be unreliable. In the Gothic, unbelievability protects what is unbelievable – the crime, the monster, the uncanny – until it becomes not just believable but undeniable. But by then it is too late. Dementia, the ultimate excuse for unbelievability, adds an extra layer of protection. One of the witches advises Judith to keep her observations to herself: 'Not being able to distinguish between what's real and what's a dream, that's a sign of dementia, and they will have you diagnosed and medicated in no time' and certainly not believed (see Figure 7).

Part of what interferes with communication between individuals with dementia and even people close to them is the jarring sense of the uncanny, of sensing strangeness in someone familiar. Familiarity can make acceptance of unstable identities difficult, especially if one's own identity is destabilised by doing so. This challenge makes a diagnosis of possession or other types of monstrosity easier to understand and even more comforting than dementia because they are clear and familiar narratives, despite the growing public awareness of dementia as

Figure 7 Judith unknowingly befriends the witches.
Source: *The Manor*, directed by Axelle Carolyn (Blumhouse Television, 2021).

---

[141] Valerie Keller, 'Children of Old Age? Infantilisation of People Living with Dementia', in Anna Anna Wanka, Tabea Freutel-Funke, Sabine Andresen, and Frank Oswald (eds.), *Linking Ages: A Dialogue between Childhood and Ageing Research* (London: Routledge, 2024), pp. 276–287.

a common disease. That a beloved parent does not recognise a grandchild is uncharted territory, and it is deeply personal. As Batch and Ryan describe it, dementia 'can become a character that eclipses the personhood', but films like *Deborah Logan* and *The Manor* suggest that the person and dementia can exist simultaneously, though that person will be changed.[142] This is the power of the uncanny, to combine contradictory elements. Its obfuscation of clear, rational definitions conflicts with medical diagnosis, which might explain some of the failed medical narratives in these films. Amelia Defalco explains that the uncanny involves 'the cohabitation of tenses, memories of a familiar past rubbing up against the strange newness of the present', and so all the Gothic narrative techniques that mirror dementia symptoms might fall into this broader concept of unsettling mixed contradictions navigated through careful reading.[143]

While dementia is marked by a failure to construct a narrative that others easily understand, *The Manor* and *Deborah Logan* suggest that the fault lies with the audience rather than the storyteller. Deborah's communication may be fragmented, nonlinear and nonsensical, but Sarah and the crew are able to piece it together by adapting their interpretive strategies. However, they only make these adjustments once they believe they're 'reading' a possession narrative rather than a dementia narrative, once they believe they're reading a *Gothic* narrative. It is, ironically, within the context of dementia rather than possession that Sarah most frequently pleads, 'Ma, you're scaring me'. Deborah nailing windows shut, attacking others and herself, digging in the garden at night: there is narrative behind these actions, even if that narrative requires Gothic methods of reading and interpretation. Similarly, Judith's grandson adapts his own interpretive strategies by spending time in the home with his grandmother, something her own daughter fails to do. He believes her and urges her to become a witch based on these Gothic reading skills.

4.4 Dementia and the Supernatural

Pathologisation of dementia anchors it to medical spaces and its 'patient' to a position of powerlessness accepted by family if not by people with dementia themselves. Despite its growing commonality and attempts at positive change from different sectors, the predominant dementia narrative is one of regression and devolution, like the stalwart threats to modernity built into the foundations of the Gothic. While people with dementia are certainly capable of learning new things and creating new memories, depending on the stage and nature of their

---

[142] Batch and Ryan, 'Dementia and Contemporary Horror', p. 767.
[143] Amelia Defalco, *Uncanny Subjects: Aging in Contemporary Narrative* (Columbus: The Ohio State University Press, 2009), p. 9.

condition, the general trend of a dementia narrative is one of decline.[144] This raises the question, what would a happy ending look like for dementia horror narratives, and is it the same ending audiences would want to see?

Audiences may relate to family members or caregivers attempting to acclimate people with dementia to these new situations, but the combined feelings of embarrassment and vulnerability conveyed by scenes of resentful dependency can interfere with 'empathy for the old person with dementia'.[145] The involvement of the supernatural in these films introduce moments of power and agency for characters struggling to adjust to the submissiveness and unreliability now expected of them because of their diagnosis. That power comes from both the symptoms of dementia and parallel Gothic elements. Ironically, becoming monstrous in response to an injustice (prey to witches) or becoming the victim of monstrosity and heroically defeating it (evil possession) are two narratives that stand to reconnect audiences to characters like Deborah or Judith so that the symptoms shared by both dementia and the supernatural can be recognised as manageable. What is clear in these films is that the condition of dementia in some way facilitates access to monstrosity (and the monster's access to the older individual), reminding audiences of the vulnerability of people with dementia to threats of all kinds, supernatural and natural, individual and systemic. The evil spirit waits so long to possess Deborah because she has been strong until now, and Judith would not have been tempted to join a witch's coven until she witnessed the treatment of nursing home residents and experienced moments of her own decline. The experiences that expose people with dementia to these supernatural threats are real. Monsters offer alternatives to these narratives of helplessness.

For the rest of this section, I turn to a third text, the German film *Old People* (2022), in which monstrosity is a direct result of outright abuse. In this film, Ella and her kids return to her childhood home for her sister's wedding, only to discover that her father has been relocated to an understaffed, poorly managed nursing home. The residents of the nursing home, resentful of their exclusion from the celebration and possessed by an 'avenging spirit', get their revenge by violently slaughtering the wedding party and everyone in the village. Lacking subtly, *Old People* is clearly a form of rape-revenge zombie movie, rape taking the form of mass neglect of the village's most disabled and vulnerable older population. The nursing home is filthy and lacking in any semblance of comfort, these scenes depicted in whites and greys. While searching for her father, Ella makes eye contact with a woman lying helpless in a bed and discovers another woman lying naked on a shower floor. One man misrecognises her as family and

---

[144] Keller, 'Children', p. 276.   [145] Yoshizaki-Gibbons, 'Ageism and Ableism', p. 289.

begs for help. When Ella expresses shock, the nurse Kim, who a moment ago had claimed she was not busy, shrugs it off and blames low staffing and insufficient resources: 'Restrained, yeah, we have to or else they'll run away, fall down, or get hurt.... Some of them lie in their own crap for hours.' Dehumanisation in this facility is extreme, making it difficult to sympathise with those who witness it and do nothing.

Old People makes explicit the parallels between ageing populations with dementia and zombie narratives, clearly mimicking these monster movies through the movements of the older people, even down to its low camera angles, silhouetted mobs, and ragged hoards (see Figure 8). Ella and her family board up the house in imitation of *Night of the Living Dead* (George A. Romero, 1968), including a scene in which arms come pouring in through an open door, bash her to the ground, and drag her out. Most of the film is full of gleeful zombies/older people in triumph as their new powers allow them to move quickly and easily in violent revenge on the younger people who made them feel, as one remarks, like animals. At the end, Ella's father emerges from his symbiosis with the hoard, and the moment is one of real emotion. The recognition of his grandchildren and heartfelt profession of his love for them, sentimental in any other context, provides a real relief of humanity set here against such unapologetic monstrosity. It is the lack of apology that works, however. In fact, this moment invites the audience to sympathise with the older people as they swap being treated as monsters for being actual monsters. *Old People* takes the uncanny experience of ageing and mistreatment of those with dementia as monstrous to the extreme, triggering a fantasy of power reversal made possible through Gothic and horror frameworks. If the typical end of a dementia narrative is 'kill or cure', or of disability narratives: 'death, institutionalization

Figure 8 One of many scenes in which old people behave like zombies.
Source: *Old People*, directed by Andy Fetscher (Constantin Television, 2022).

(which serves as a metaphor for death), or cure',[146] then this film introduces another possibility that subverts the power structures of the others: revenge.

The clear lesson to treat older people with respect and kindness (or they will murder you) is achieved with the classic zombie reminder that the monster is us and we are the monsters. Narratives of ageing are our own, as might be narratives of dementia. The older man begging Ella for help later hands her a scrap of paper – a complete fragment – that reads 'thou shalt honour the old for they are great in number, and one day you will all be like them'. This is a plea not just to care for family members but to protect the ageing in general. While defending themselves, Ella's ex-husband says to one of them, 'you're angry at somebody, and maybe they treated you badly, but it certainly wasn't us'. Clearly, the lesson of the film is lost on its characters. While stressing the graphically poor conditions of the nursing home, the film also points to systemic problems. When the crime is neglect – a lack of care from an absent staff – it is not easy to point fingers. The attack on the entire village implies they are all complicit in a system to which they will eventually fall prey themselves. Ironically, killing them when they are younger spares them that end. Thomas Kitwood, in his work on personhood discussed more in the next section, lays out a series of 'malignant elements' that dehumanise people with dementia: treachery, disempowerment, infantilisation, intimidation, labelling, stigmatisation, outpacing, invalidation, banishment, and objectification.[147] However, he is careful to clarify that the term 'malignant' does not 'imply evil intent on the part of caregivers; most of their work is done with kindness and good intent. The malignancy is part of our cultural inheritance'.[148] While the staff in *Old People* can hardly claim good intent, let alone kindness, Kitwood's point speaks to the film's approach to justice: a cultural inheritance can (or should) become a cultural curse.

At the end of each film, defeating the monster does not mean defeating dementia; they are not the same. While each film reaches a resolution, there is no real sense that progress has been made, either for dementia care or for defeating supernatural threats more broadly. But, the audience will leave the cinema still fearing one more than the other. Characters who held great power for a brief time have lost it again as they return to their diseased states. In *The Manor*, Judith does maintain her supernatural power, but only by devouring the energy of the home's residents as hers was once devoured. In fact, each film adopts the dangerous attitude that, though dementia is the lesser evil, ending the

---

[146] Yoshizaki-Gibbons, 'Ageism and Ableism', p. 287.
[147] Thomas Kitwood, *Dementia Reconsidered, Revisited: The Person Still Comes First*, 2nd Ed., Dawn Brooker (ed.) (London: Open University Press, 2019), p. 52.
[148] Kitwood, *Dementia Reconsidered, Revisited*, p. 52.

life of someone experiencing age-related cognitive decline is 'a mercy', an attitude that contributes to stigma far more than zombies, witches, or demonic possession.

5 Uncanny Connections: Caregivers and Caretakers

Conflating dementia – and mental illness in general – with the supernatural, while empowering, can also prevent direct access to the dementia experience by making it seem irrational and unsympathetic. As people with dementia may struggle to communicate the details of their experience, and as their reliance on nonnormative, nonlinear narrative structures to do so often discredits them, the combination both makes sense and becomes dangerously misleading. Deborah Logan is clearly levitating and eating children because she is possessed, not because she has dementia, *but* it takes the length of the film and the willingness of her daughter to interpret her mother's narrative using Gothic methods to learn this. In contrast, the films discussed in this section either eschew the supernatural altogether or extend the supernatural beyond the dementia experience to include caregivers, both professionals and family members. This is a crucial difference in how they apply Gothic narrative elements, to not just isolate by pushing dementia symptoms to a supernatural, unbelievable extreme, but to share those impossible experiences with caregivers, whom the audience is more likely to believe. This transfers the burden of belief to the audience, calling into question why symptoms of dementia are so easily dismissed that the supernatural is easier to believe than a person with dementia.

By extending the disorienting experience of the supernatural to the audience by proxy of the caregivers, these films essentially confront them with their own assumptions about dementia and credibility. If characters without dementia and audience members can encounter unbelievable supernatural incidents and react to them as if real, then that same suspension of disbelief might produce sympathy, even empathy, for people with dementia whose symptoms produce similar real reactions to and real beliefs about confused realities. In short, these characters model a habit of belief. In conversation with the previous section about dementia's resemblance to a supernatural curse or possession, this section examines instances when these same supernatural symptoms become shared experiences, alleviating the weight of that experience falling exclusively on the shoulders of individuals with dementia. Shared unbelievable experiences call attention to both the distress of self-doubt and the frustration of caregiving within a culture that privileges individualism over community. The films discussed in this section demonstrate the value of the supernatural to disrupt confidence in reality, to require belief in the unbelievable, and to abandon the concepts of both dehumanisation and humanisation in favour of something bigger found through posthumanist readings. Two of these films include elements of the shared supernatural – *Relic* (Natalie Erika James, 2020) and *The Rule of Jenny Pen* (James Ashcroft, 2025) – and two exclude the supernatural to explore dementia and caregiving as Gothic experiences on their own – *Dementia* (Mike Testin, 2015) and *The Visit* (M. Night Shyamalan, 2015).

5.1 Family Caregivers: The Sins of the Parent (and Grandparent)

Many critics have remarked on the growing number of films depicting older populations and characters with dementia.[149] There is no mystery as to why this is occurring as the Baby Boomer generation gets older and an increasing number will experience dementia symptoms, with or without a formal diagnosis. According to the Alzheimer's Association and Alzheimer's Society, over a million people in the United Kingdom and over seven million in the United States had been diagnosed with Alzheimer's disease as of 2024, while the World Health Organization lists fifty-five to fifty-seven million people with dementia worldwide as of 2021.[150] With numbers rising, so too are fears that older populations may overrun medical facilities, draining them of already strained resources and impacting the quality of care for those who manage to obtain it. Along with the many fears associated with dementia in this Element are those of loss of independence and the need to depend on socio-economic safety nets that may not exist: healthcare, mobility assistance, transportation, and guidance navigating changing technologies required to fulfil basic needs. Dementia is not a biosocial death, but many fear it is. In a culture that emphasises freedom and independence, the loss of independence is daunting on a practical level alone.

Fears of medical intervention into patient identity and independence discussed in the previous sections are at the root of the history of dementia studies and the personhood approach led by Tom Kitwood in the 1990s. According to Kitwood, personhood is 'a standing or status that is bestowed upon one human being, by others, in the context of relationship and social being. It implies recognition, respect and trust'.[151] In the context of dementia, he targets circumstances that produce 'a particular kind of inhumanity: a social psychology that is

---

[149] See Chivers, *The Silvering Screen*; Keetley, 'The Shock'.
[150] WHO, 'Dementia'; Alzheimer's Society, 'Facts for the Media about Dementia, *Alzheimer's Society*, 13 May 2024, www.alzheimers.org.uk/about-us/news-and-media/facts-media [last accessed 22 June 2025]; Alzheimer's Association, 'Alzheimer's Disease Facts and Figures', *Alzheimer's Association*, 2025, www.alz.org/alzheimers-dementia/facts-figures [last accessed 22 June 2025].
[151] Kitwood, *Dementia Reconsidered, Revisited*, p. 7.

malignant in its effects, even when it proceeds from people who are kind and well-intentioned', and he attributes this to widespread anxieties about physical and mental frailties.[152] This fear of encountering our future selves leads to not just abuse but also dehumanisation, turning people with dementia 'into a different species'. Only when the anxieties that lead to such fraught interactions are addressed can people with dementia receive care as humans.[153] Kitwood's theories clearly laid important foundations for patient advocacy, particularly in medicalised dementia care, and dementia studies still shares these values. However, the turn to *critical* dementia studies led to concerns about Kitwood's claim that humanity must be 'bestowed'[154] by external actors and that he focused on individual cases at the expense of the cultural factors that create them.[155] Without disagreeing with these criticisms, I suggest that the films in this section demonstrate a continued need for the spirit of Kitwood's theories while also challenging personhood as needed for inherent worth and care.

Institutional care, despite arguments to the contrary, still bears associations with abuse, including medical facilities, nursing homes, or professional live-in care.[156] This type of abusive relationship is at the centre of the film *Dementia* (2015), in which George has developed dementia from a stroke. Estranged from his family other than a granddaughter, he begrudgingly accepts help from a nurse who becomes increasingly abusive, both mentally and physically. In *The Rule of Jenny Pen* (2025), similar types of abuse occur through neglect but also unchecked bullying from other patients. A judge who has no family has a stroke that leaves him disabled and in a nursing home, where he and other residents are tormented by another resident with a sinister puppet. Neither George nor the judge has any recourse to defend himself as physical and mental abilities decline throughout the films. In contrast, *The Visit* (2015) subverts possible abuse when the patients fight back and escape from the hospital, killing and then posing as the estranged grandparents who flaunted a family the patients would never have themselves.

The concept of personhood, then, rightly focuses on medical relationships and problematic medical discourse, but most dementia care today is managed

---

[152] Kitwood, *Dementia Reconsidered, Revisited*, p.11.
[153] Kitwood, *Dementia Reconsidered, Revisited*, p. 11.
[154] Fletcher, *The Biopolitics*, pp. 32–33.
[155] Jan Dewing, 'Commentary: On Being a Person', in Dawn Brooker (ed.), *Dementia Reconsidered, Revisited: The Person Still Comes First* (London: Open University Press, 2019), pp. 17–23.
[156] Lucy Burke, 'On (Not) Caring: Tracing the Meanings of Care in the Imaginative Literature of the "Alzheimer's Epidemic"', in Anne Whitehead and Angela Woods (eds.), *The Edinburgh Companion to the Critical Medical Humanities* (Edinburgh: Edinburgh University Press, 2016), pp. 596–610.

informally outside these medical spaces, underdiagnosed and undertreated in primary care settings. Diagnosis and treatment are still considered to be crucial for improved outcomes, but symptoms may be misrepresented by patients, families, and other interested parties like insurance companies.[157] What is considered 'normal' in terms of ageing and daily functions remains undefined and encourages a reliance on anecdotal evidence to initiate the diagnosis process. Some of that evidence must come from those who would notice whether a behaviour is 'normal' or not, instilling even well-intentioned family and friends with the unwanted power to pathologise. In the United States, 83 per cent of assistance for ageing populations, including those with dementia, is provided by family members or unpaid volunteers. The average lifetime cost of this care in the United States is estimated to be $405,262 as of 2024, and 70 per cent of that cost is born by the family.[158] Some argue that this is by design, as informal and often unrecognised unpaid labour relieves pressure on the formal and funded safety nets that capitalist societies are loathe to provide.[159] The ambiguous nature of dementia as a disease so little understood, even amidst impressive medical advancements, trickles down to insufficient guidance for when and how family members should seek or provide care.

Medical participation in the films discussed here is limited to assessment. These scenes range from the cold and harrowing depictions of physical and mental exams in *The Rule of Jenny Pen* to the intimate and friendly in-house check-up in *Relic* after matriarch Edna has disappeared for a few days and then reappears on her own. Her daughter Kay and granddaughter Sam are called in to search for her and, after the doctor declares Edna should not be alone for a few weeks because of a mysterious bruise on her chest, they discover her progressing dementia and begin to explore options for long-term care. Edna's symptoms include mood swings, trouble remembering, increased fear of home invasion, delusions of intruders, and eventually self-harm. Unlike Deborah Logan, Edna is not clearly possessed by an evil spirit, but her bruise does become increasingly supernatural. Eager to get back to work, Kay visits a nursing home like the one inhabited by the judge in *The Rule of Jenny Pen*, but the sterile environment and wide array of accessibility devices make her doubt whether Edna is 'ready for

---

[157] Ladson Hinton, Yvette Fores, Carol Franz, Isabel Hernandez, and Linda S. Mitteness, 'The Borderlands of Primary Care Physician and Family Perspectives on "Troublesome" Behaviors of People with Dementia', in Annette Leibing and Lawrence Cohen (eds.), *Thinking about Dementia: Culture, Loss, and the Anthropology of Senility* (New Brunswick: Rutgers University Press, 2006), pp. 43–63 (pp. 44–45).

[158] Alzheimer's Association, 'Alzheimer's Disease Facts'.

[159] Katherine Ludwin, '"On my good days, I can [...] almost pass for a normal person": Reading the Film *Still Alice* Using the Conceptual Lens of Heteronormativity', in James Rupert Fletcher and Andrea Capstick (eds.), *A Critical History of Dementia Studies* (London: Routledge, 2024), pp. 95–109 (p. 97).

a place like this', despite the staff's instance that it is 'five-star living'. Joining the large percentage of unpaid family caregivers becomes increasingly necessary for Kay and Sam. Viewers might be expected to relate to caregivers over characters with dementia since so many in the audience may be caregivers themselves or anticipate filling that role in the future. It is not surprising that at least 70 per cent of care is provided by women[160] and over a third of caregivers are daughters.[161] In almost all the films discussed in this Element, daughters and especially granddaughters are the main defenders of characters with dementia. As in life, these adult children struggle with decisions about the best way to care for a parent while maintaining their own careers and supporting their own children, a growing position sometimes referred to as the 'sandwich generation'.

Becoming a family caregiver may, of course, provide fulfilment and valuable time with loved ones, but it can also cause confusion, frustration, and distress. Like Kay, many adult children must face their own uncanny relationship reversal as a once independent and dependable parent becomes unreliable and dependent. Sudden responsibility and uncertainty make these characters seem irritable and cold as they navigate the practicalities of care and of suddenly becoming the enforcer of rules they perhaps once faced as a child. This altered relationship is hard on Kay. The most repeated word throughout *Relic* is 'Mum', continually complicating that relationship as the identity it implies shifts throughout the film, creating both a doubling of identity (it applies to both Edna and Kay) but also a slipperiness as an identity that can be acquired or lost. Does Edna always recognise herself in that role? In searching the woods for Edna, most participants call her name, but Kay calls for 'Mum', just as Sarah called for 'Ma' during a similar scene in *Deborah Logan*. The repeated word is a constant reminder of traditional caregiving relationships and how dementia reverses them. Unlike Sam, Kay talks more *about* Edna than *to* her, other than to repeatedly ask, 'what are you doing?' as her mother's actions confuse and unsettle her. It is an accusation more than a question, so she rarely receives an answer. In response to Kay's frustration, Sam asks, 'Isn't that how it works: your mum changes your nappies, and you change hers?' and eventually offers to move in with Edna since she is much less invested in systems of capitalistic productivity than her mother is.

Kay and Sam's two reactions illustrate different approaches in dementia care, both well intentioned: sending Edna away as a sick patient to be safely dealt with by others or fully embracing her as a sacrifice of one's own independence. Kay largely adheres to the medical model of dementia, interpreting the disease as a problem, focusing on what Edna can no longer do, and diminishing her

---

[160] WHO, 'Dementia'.   [161] Alzheimer's Association, 'Alzheimer's Disease Facts'.

status as an individual with agency to make meaning. Sam, on the other hand, demonstrates Kitwood's personhood model, which 'insists that in interpersonal relations people with dementia interact as proper agents whose preferences, well-being, and reactions matter'.[162] Characters with dementia in horror tend to reject both approaches as patronising, however, albeit in different ways. In *The Rule of Jenny Pen*, the residents show that the staff do not have the power to keep them safe from one another, let alone bestow any kind of care or personhood on them. In *The Visit*, the counterfeit grandparents express their rejection of any assistance by escaping the hospital and redefining themselves completely and convincingly until the end. Similarly, in *Dementia*, George subverts every attempt to establish the sympathy of his granddaughter when he confesses to the brutal rape and murder of his 'evil' nurse's mother in the last minutes of the film, a total rejection of the selfhood his granddaughter attempted to bestow on him and a rewrite of who the audience thought he was. Attempts to sentimentalise these characters because they have dementia will be doomed to fail in the Gothic. Edna insists that she is 'not a project', that she has no need to rely on her daughter or granddaughter to define what or who she is. Not only do characters with dementia demonstrate the Gothic's insistence on unreliable identities, they also do so in ways that challenge power relationships, especially those that determine who deserved care and why.

5.2 The Shared Supernatural: Personhood and Posthumanism

One of the most difficult aspects of navigating dementia narratives is the inaccessibility of the dementia experience for those outside it. While previous sections have demonstrated the narrative elements that resemble dementia symptoms and the approaches readers take to interpret them, the barrier between 'healthy' and 'unhealthy' and 'real' and 'unreal' remains problematically obstructive. Bryden writes that 'Recognizing my continuing sense of being an embodied self within dementia is important for those on the outside, so that they can regard me as having a valid subjective perspective, which is my insider's view, giving new insights into the lived experience of dementia'.[163] The reality is that most people with dementia *do* depend on others to recognise their humanity in order to survive, and that interaction relies on fairly narrow definitions of humanity that include coherent communication and memory-based self-awareness. In the previous section, the use of the supernatural demonstrated the difficulties of interpreting dementia as an outsider. Rather than bringing the experience of dementia to those outsiders and relying on their limited interpretive capabilities, the films in this section use the supernatural to

---

[162] Vermeulen, 'Infrastructures of Aging', p. 17.   [163] Bryden, 'Will I Still', p. 62.

bring outsiders *into* the dementia experience, where they must interpret and react as it becomes their own. The supernatural, then, facilitates the 'reconfiguration of cognition and agency' that Bruce Jennings suggests can keep people with dementia in 'this world': 'But this adaptation is not and cannot be achieved solely by the individual alone.'[164] *Relic* and *The Rule of Jenny Pen* (and *The Visit* and *Dementia* to a lesser extent) shift the burden of believability from the disadvantaged position of someone with dementia to the relative authority position of those who care for them, giving the caregiver and the audience no choice but to share the world of belief with them or to doubt themselves.

Relic and *Jenny Pen* use Gothic elements to subvert stable notions of identity, space, and time to bring outsiders into the dementia experience, but they are not the first to attempt or value this approach. A well-known short Scottish training video, 'Darkness in the Afternoon' (1999) repositions the audience from the external position of observer to the internal perspective of someone experiencing dementia symptoms: a woman in a red dress is approached by an older stranger, and all attempts to escape this man fail as everyone around her helps him to capture and imprison her in an unfamiliar house. At the end, she encounters a mirror reflection of an unknown older woman, a terrifying experience for her and the audience. Nicole Matthews traces the Gothic storytelling techniques and effects that emphasise the horror of the woman's situation but also the ways in which this approach shows caregivers and family members how threatening they can become to a person with dementia, reversing the position of monstrous Other from the person with dementia to their caregivers. Everyone has a role in the story, and the video prompts rethinking that role from a Gothic perspective.[165]

Films that dissolve the antagonistic line separating caregivers from those for whom they care suggest an interconnectivity of those roles and the artificiality of hierarchies based on their stability. Like the use of Gothic tropes in 'Darkness in the Afternoon', the supernatural in *Jenny Pen* and *Relic* dismantles the isolation of the dementia position by transforming it into a shared experience, which falls within a third approach to dementia alongside medical and personhood: de-centring humanism or posthumanism. Katz and Leibing, who see the development of dementia studies in stages, describe the stage after Kitwood's person-centred care as 'de-centring humanism', a 'deconstruction of normative forms of selfhood and identity associated with taken-for-granted expectations of

---

[164] Bruce Jennings, 'Cognition and Recognition in the Ethics of Dementia Care', in Marlene Goldman Kate de Medeiros and Thomas Cole (eds.), *Critical Humanities and Aging: Forging Interdisciplinary Dialogues* (London: Routledge, 2022), pp. 58–70 (p. 62).

[165] Nicole Matthews, 'Learning to Listen: Epistemic Injustice and Gothic Film in Dementia Care Education', *Feminist Media Studies* 16.6 (2016): 1078–1092 (pp. 1079–1085).

continuity in time' such that those forms cannot be used to determine worth.[166] Here, de-centred humanism or posthumanism echoes a Gothic approach, disrupting reliance on static identities and human exceptionalism. While the Gothic may come from a place of transgressed boundaries and instabilities, posthumanism more specifically promotes the practice of calling out dehumanisation while also expanding value beyond humanism – especially individualised humanism – as a privileged category. In other words, whether an individual is human or not human is irrelevant; they do not need to be human to deserve care. Posthumanism would suggest that commitment to countering dehumanisation alone, while well-intentioned, limits progress because the definition of human is itself limited to a system built on exclusion rather than inclusion.[167] As Katz and Leibing describe, 'to undo and to make, to un-become and to become, to create and to alter memory, to live in a multitude of temporal flows ... is a way of de-centring the limits of purely humanist personhood',[168] disturbing acts that Gothic conventions and narrative strategies regularly perform. Posthumanism suggests not that humans do not matter but that value should be extended and allow for a multiplicity of forms, networks, and existences in addition to humans.

In dementia horror, the supernatural furthers the ends of posthumanism by dismantling rational understandings of time, space, and individuality, calling humanity into question in ways that blur its defining lines for both those with dementia and their caregivers. It does this by extending the limits of the supernatural experience beyond the person with dementia to encompass others through a shared experience of the anger, confusion, and fear typically experienced by and used to dehumanise those with dementia. Supernatural occurrences confined to characters with dementia make it easy for the audience to causally wonder what is real and what is not. When those experiences occur for multiple characters or are shown to the audience, the line between delusion and reality becomes less clear but also less important. In *The Rule of Jenny Pen*, the slow introduction of the supernatural carefully brings the audience into it. The audience sees this world from the perspective of the judge, from the low camera angles of his wheelchair to the abrupt scene breaks and repeated images. Film audiences are used to being picked up and dropped in and out of scenes as part of cinematic storytelling, but it becomes clear that this view also represents the judge's unfiltered experience of losing awareness and memory. When the

---

[166] Katz and Leibing, '"Lost in Time"', p. 64.

[167] Nick Jenkins, 'Multi-Species Dementia Studies: How Moving Beyond Human Exceptionalism Can Advance Dementia's More Critical Turn', in Richard Ward and Linn J. Sandberg (eds.), *Critical Dementia Studies: An Introduction* (London: Routledge, 2023), pp. 72–82 (p. 74).

[168] Katz and Leibing, 'Lost in Time', p. 65.

abusive puppet begins to change in subtle ways, it is not immediately clear whether they are real or part of the judge's delusion until they become increasingly impossible. The sparsity of characters in these scenes to contribute frame of reference adds to audience uncertainty. What is certain, however, is that the judge is experiencing these visions as real, and his progressing dementia spreads to the audience. As these scenes extend validity beyond the rational human, posthumanism also extends the *human* beyond the human, 'not as a master but as a being existing in a relationship with other beings [which] implies profoundly reconceptualizing the way we think of humans and animals, and their shared ontologies and worlds', as Zahi Zalloua writes.[169] The supernatural in these films makes existing networks and interdependencies visible, showing that humans already exist beyond themselves. A shared experience of the supernatural is no longer just a dementia delusion, and the emotions and reactions to it must be acknowledge as real and valid because they also become our own.

In *Relic*, similar experiences are extended not just to the audience but to characters considered to be healthy and reliable. Kay accuses Edna of needing help because she finds locks and notes all over the house, physical evidence of Edna's growing worry about intruders that she readily voices herself. Aside from the fact that Edna is a single woman living in a remote area, the addition of the supernatural suggests she might be right to worry, disrupting the easy disbelief many with dementia face. Early on, Sam shares Edna's experience, hearing noises and seeing things in Edna's house, even when Edna is not home. Sam goes into a closet that goes on and on, shifting into hallways that get smaller and darker, as shown in Figure 9. She breaks through the walls, only to find more hallways. The house is changing, or Sam is changing, or Edna is changing and bringing her sympathetic granddaughter with her. Sam's panic grows as she finds notes – fragments – that refer equally to Edna's memories and to something sinister in the house. The uncanny dementia experience is not isolating or isolated here as it becomes unclear which is more horrifying: the fact that Edna has been reporting an 'actual' threat or that Sam is sharing in Edna's cognitive decline. A Gothic lens might suggest that both scenarios are the same: Edna's experience is an actual occurrence for her, and the posthumanism of this scene reduces barriers that restrict it to herself. That she shares it with Sam also makes that insight accessible to an audience too ready to take their cues from the 'healthier' characters.

---

[169] Zahi Zalloua, 'Posthumanism', in Jeffrey R. Di Leo (ed.), *The Bloomsbury Handbook of Literary and Cultural Theory* (London: Bloomsbury, 2018), pp. 310–322 (p. 314).

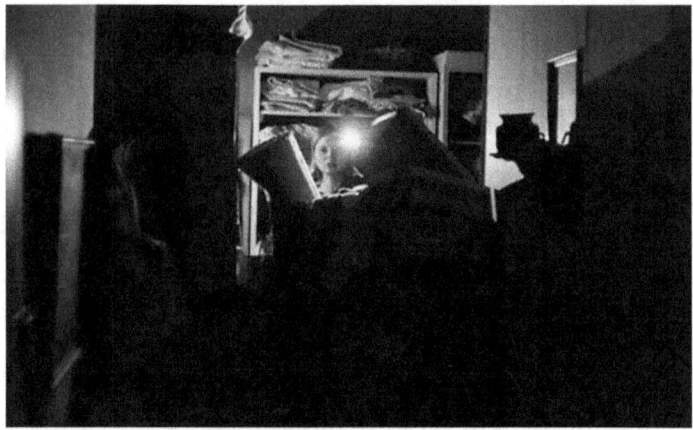

Figure 9 Sam ventures into the impossible expanding and twisting closet.
Source: *Relic*, directed by Natalie Erika James (Nine Stories Productions, 2020).

At the same time that Sam and Kay constantly evaluate Edna throughout the film, occasionally using the language of Otherness when she becomes an unrecognisable stranger to them, people with dementia also express doubt in the identities of people they should know. As 'Darkness in the Afternoon' demonstrates, Otherness can be ascribed to both parties. All three women in *Relic* have multiple identities in relation to one another – mum, gran, daughter, granddaughter – that get shuffled and reshuffled and eventually doubted. Edna proudly recites Sam's birthday when the doctor checks her cognitive health, but later she not only does not recognise her but suspects she is an imposter: 'they look like Kay and Sammy but it's not them. They're pretending', she says to herself, and she directly accuses, 'You're not Kay. I don't know you'. Though this is likely the dementia interfering with her cognitive processing, she could also mean this metaphorically: just as her family claims to not know her, this could double as a recognition of changes in her daughter and granddaughter in response to her dementia. This woman who values her career over her mother is not her daughter. This woman who tells her that Kay is looking into nursing homes is not her granddaughter. These women who hurt her cannot be her family. Caregivers may not realise that their identities also change, and not just because people with dementia struggle to remember them. In *Relic*, this dehumanising Otherness dissipates as identities buckle and collapse. Unable to trust who is whom, the family transcends both the medical and the personhood approaches once the house and Edna begin to transform, challenging them to de-centre the human or lose Edna completely.

In bridging the divide between individual subjectivities, the posthumanist approach to navigating dementia in *Relic* takes advantage of the supernatural and unstable identities that characterise the Gothic. Near the end of the film, Kay insists to Sam, 'Mum is not, it's not her anymore'. Except that Edna is herself, just a self with dementia, which transgresses humanism's limited view of what a self is and what it can be. Kay's statement is important, however, because, first, it echoes the unsettling difficulties at the root of caring for a parent in physical and cognitive transition: the devotion to only one, unchangeable version of a person based on memories of a past self that can never be restored. Fear of losing one's self is commonly expressed by those with early diagnoses or who have a family history of cognitive disease, a fear that loss of memory precedes additional losses: selfhood, independence, connection. But, second, Kay's statement contrasts with her adoption of a more flexible approach just moments later, modelling the possibility of recognising dementia as more than loss and deficit, to discover possibility in what remains. Rather than leaving her mother, Kay decides to stay.

In contrast, *The Visit* follows a more traditional horror film structure, teasing progressive if disturbing concepts but defeating them at the end. Teenagers Becca and Tyler attempt to connect with their fake grandparents by accepting the older people's need for help. Becca explains away every strange act as simply another sign of dementia and more generally, 'They're old', suggesting that age itself may have posthumanising powers. Yet, *The Visit* also plays on fears of Otherness and lost connection. At first, the grandparents are kind and warm, making the kids feel at home by sharing family stories. Becca even remarks that she and Nana have the same eyes. However, the film exaggerates and rewards the common dementia fear of family becoming strangers when it reveals the grandparents are actual strangers: escaped patients who murdered the real grandparents. Once this is revealed, not only are they no longer family, they become no longer human. While both films depict moments of humanisation, *The Visit* ultimately dehumanises while *Relic* posthumanises. Posthumanism insists that selfhood and independence are the delusion and that connection can only be lost when reliant upon them as unchanging entities. Fletcher writes that 'posthumanist dementia studies contests the existence of the person as an individually unified, rigidly demarcated and self-contained entity.... As well as being composite, the person is also symbiotic, entailing profound interdependence with a range of other entities, human, animal, mechanical, digital and so on'.[170] Independence, in other words, uneasily rests on

---

[170] Fletcher, *The Biopolitics*, p. 39.

unseen systems of dependence and interdependence, which the Gothic lies bare by disrupting the boundaries between self and other.

5.3 Conclusion

The boundaries of space, identity, individuality, and finally time have begun to dissolve by the time Edna transforms into a supernatural humanoid creature of bruise and mould, embodying the posthuman as both recognisably and arguably *not* human at the same time. Having been through the impossible house and witnessed Edna's violence, Kay fights back to protect her own daughter. But even these acts of violence cannot repair the barriers designating separate selves. As she turns to leave, Edna calls Kay back by her name, simultaneously re-establishing the connection Kay has always had to Edna, as her daughter. The past, present, and future merge in this moment, just as the three women are and always have been each other. Posthumanist dementia studies privileges 'transcending anthropocentric ideas and conceiving the person with dementia as entangled in embodied, relational or more-than-human relations and environments'.[171] Despite Sam's pleas to Kay that 'it's not Gran anymore', Kay discards the need to recognise that it is or is not her mother, insisting that she 'can't leave her', a noticeable transformation from the woman ready to commit Edna to a nursing home so she could return to work.

Simultaneously recognising her human connection with her mother and her posthuman connection with a living being in need of care, divorced from time and space, Kay also transcends her own independence and humanity. As Anya Heise-von der Lippe writes, 'the posthuman Gothic makes us aware that the monstrous Other is not only lodged with, but an essential part of our (human) identity construction'.[172] Kay's obligations to her job, her life as an individual, even her daughter are totally forgotten. This silent scene becomes a transformation of all three bodies into a new relationship through the monstrous Otherness of Edna's dementia now become totally familiar. Tenderly removing Edna's clothes, then her bruised skin, Kay now no longer even requires Edna to fall within the strict definition of 'Edna', let alone the strict definition of human, to care for her. Kissing her and lying in the bed behind her, Kay is joined by Sam, who lies behind her mother, as seen in Figure 11. In noticing the beginning of a bruise identical to Edna's on Kay's back, Sam sees the future for them all. Dehumanisation, neglect, abuse, and stigma directed towards people with dementia all speak to an illogical inability to connect the

---

[171] Katz and Leibing, 'Lost in Time', p. 66.
[172] Anya Heise-von der Lippe, 'Introduction: Post/human/Gothic', in Anya Heise-von der Lippe (ed.), *Posthuman Gothic* (Cardiff: University of Wales Press, 2017), pp. 1–16 (p. 6).

Figure 10 Edna, Kay, and Sam share the experience of dementia.
Source: *Relic*, directed by Natalie Erika James (Nine Stories Productions, 2020).

present to a potential future that could include dementia for every young and healthy person. For a cultural understanding of dementia stigma that invests so much in coherent, temporal narratives, the failure to anticipate this realistic chronological end to the story – that any one of us could face dementia in our future – is its own type of delusion. It speaks to the unexpected usefulness of Gothic modes and narrative techniques to reveal the disturbing connections between not just people with dementia and their caregivers but all humans with ageing and unstable bodies and minds. That is, all humans.

In an interview about her portrayal of Kay in *Relic*, Emily Mortimer noted that she wanted to 'really sum up the essence of the experience [of decline and death] emotionally. And if it helps someone process the experience in a new way or helps them conquer that fear, that would be pretty amazing'.[173] A genre and a narrative tradition known for its commitment to entertainment and accused of revelling in pain, suffering, and gore while corrupting readers and contributing to stigma *also* offers invaluable insight into the fears that direct our reactions to dementia. A Gothic approach to the undeniable changes occasioned by dementia encourages not just accepting but also supporting what those with dementia and all those connected with them are becoming. This requires a loosened grasp on preconceived notions of identity and coherent communication. Acknowledging the unpredictability and changeability of the human experience may be an approach the Gothic can facilitate: witnessing, exposing, empowering, and providing a framework for suspending disbelief and navigating unconventional forms of meaning that expand acceptance of the human experience as often incoherent, monstrous, frightening, and connected.

---

[173] Sonaiya Kelley, 'Emily Mortimer Explains the "Extraordinary and Bizarre" Ending of "Relic"', *Los Angeles Times*, 10 July 2020, www.latimes.com/entertainment-arts/movies/story/2020-07-10/relic-ending-explained-emily-mortimer[last accessed 22 June 2025].

Bibliography

Aiken, John and Anna Letitia Barbauld, 'Sir Bertrand, A Fragment', in E. J. Clery and Robert Miles (eds.), *Gothic Documents: A Sourcebook, 1700–1820* (Manchester: Manchester University Press, 2000), pp. 130–132.

Alzheimer's Association, 'Alzheimer's Disease Facts and Figures', *Alzheimer's Association*, 2025, www.alz.org/alzheimers-dementia/facts-figures [last accessed 22 June 2025].

Alzheimer's Disease International, 'World's Largest Dementia Study Reveals Two Thirds of People Still Incorrectly Think Dementia is a Normal Part of Ageing, Rather Than a Medical Condition', *Alzheimer's Disease International*, 1 September 2019, www.alzint.org/news-events/news/worlds-largest-dementia-study-reveals-two-thirds-of-people-still-incorrectly-think-dementia-is-a-normal-part-of-ageing-rather-than-a-medical-condition/ [last accessed 21 June 2025].

Alzheimer Society, 'The Differences between Normal Aging and Dementia', *Alzheimer's Society: Canada*, https://alzheimer.ca/en/about-dementia/do-i-have-dementia/differences-between-normal-aging-dementia [last accessed 21 June 2025].

Alzheimer's Society, 'Facts for the Media about Dementia', *Alzheimer's Society*, 13 May 2024, www.alzheimers.org.uk/about-us/news-and-media/facts-media [last accessed 22 June 2025].

Baldick, Chris, 'Introduction', in Chris Baldick (ed.), *The Oxford Book of Gothic Tales* (Oxford: Oxford University Press, 2009), pp. xi–xxiii.

Ballenger, Jesse, 'Dementia: Confusion at the Borderlands of Aging and Madness', in Greg Eghigian (ed.), *The Routledge History of Madness and Mental Health* (London: Routledge, 2017), pp. 297–311.

Batch, Morgan and Mark David Ryan, 'Dementia and Contemporary Horror Movies: Gendered Ageing and the Haunted Home', *New Review of Film and Television Studies* 22.3 (2024): 760–780.

Braun, Joanna, *Performing Hysteria: Images and Imaginations of Hysteria* (Leuven: Leuven University Press, 2020).

Brooker, Dawn, 'Person-Centred Dementia Care: The Legacy of Tom Kitwood', *International Journal of Percent-Centred Medicine* 12. 2 (2022): 21–36.

Bryden, Christine, *Will I Still Be Me? Finding a Continuing Sense of Self in the Lived Experience of Dementia* (London: Jessica Kingsley, 2018).

Buhuniak, Susan M., 'The Living Dead? The Construction of People with Alzheimer's Disease as Zombies', *Ageing & Society* 31 (2011): 70–92.

Burke, Lucy, 'Missing Pieces: Trauma, Dementia and the Ethics of Reading in Elizabeth is Missing', in Tess Maginess (ed.), *Dementia and Literature: Interdisciplinary Perspectives* (London: Routledge, 2019), pp. 88–102.

Burke, Lucy, 'On (Not) Caring: Tracing the Meanings of Care in the Imaginative Literature of the "Alzheimer's Epidemic"', in Anne Whitehead and Angela Woods (eds.), *The Edinburgh Companion to the Critical Medical Humanities* (Edinburgh: Edinburgh University Press, 2016), pp. 596–610.

Burke, Lucy, 'Spectres of Unproductive Life', in Katie Aubrecht, Christine Kelly, and Carla Rice (eds.), *The Aging-Disability Nexus* (Toronto: UBC Press, 2020), pp. 35–50.

Capstick, Andrea, 'The Century without a War: Kitwood's Concept of Malignant Social Psychology and the Need for Historicisation in Dementia Studies', in James Rupert Fletcher and Andrea Capstick (eds.), *A Critical History of Dementia Studies* (London: Routledge, 2024), pp. 27–37.

CDC, 'About Dementia', *CDC: Alzheimer's Disease and Dementia*, 17 August 2024, www.cdc.gov/alzheimers-dementia/about/index.html [last accessed 20 June 2025].

CDC, 'Signs and Symptoms of Dementia', *CDC: Alzheimer's Disease and Dementia*, 14 August 2025, www.cdc.gov/alzheimers-dementia/signs-symptoms/index.html [last accessed 20 June 2025].

Charise, Andrea, '"The Tyranny of Age": Godwin's *St. Leon* and the Nineteenth-Century Longevity Narrative', *ELH* 79:4 (Winter 2012): 905–933.

Chivers, Sally, *The Silvering Screen: Old Age and Disability in Cinema* (Toronto: University of Toronto Press, 2011).

Christ, Susanne Katharina, *Fictions of Dementia: Narrative Modes of Presenting Dementia in Anglophone Novels* (Berlin: De Gruyter, 2022).

Coleridge, Samuel Taylor, 'Biographia Literaria; or Biographical Sketches of my Literary Life and Opinions', in Joseph Black, Leonard Conolly, Kate Flint et al. (eds.), *The Broadview Anthology of Romantic Poetry* (Peterborough: Broadview Press, 2016), pp. 560–573.

Coleridge, Samuel Taylor, 'Kubla Khan, Or, A Vision in a Dream: A Fragment', in Joseph Black, Leonard Conolly, Kate Flint et al. (eds.), *The Broadview Anthology of Romantic Poetry* (Peterborough: Broadview Press, 2016), pp. 556–557.

Coleridge, Samuel Taylor, *The Rime of the Ancient Mariner*, edited by Paul H. Fry (Boston: Bedford/St. Martin's, 1999).

Commisso, Elana, 'The Zero-Degree of Dementia: Thinking the Gap between Subject and Substance', in Aagje Swinnen and Mark Schweda (eds.), *Popularizing Dementia: Public Expressions and Representations of Forgetfulness* (New York: Columbia University Press, 2016), pp. 377–401.

Defalco, Amelia, *Uncanny Subjects: Aging in Contemporary Narrative* (Columbus: The Ohio State University Press, 2009).

Dementia, directed by Mike Testin (BoulderLight Pictures, 2015).

Dewing, Jan, 'Commentary: On Being a Person', in Dawn Brooker (ed.), *Dementia Reconsidered, Revisited: The Person Still Comes First* (London: Open University Press, 2019), pp. 17–23.

Dickens, Charles, *Great Expectations* (New York: Signet Classic, 1980).

Esquirol, Jean Étienne Dominique, *Mental Maladies: A Treatise on Insanity*, trans. E. K. Hunt (Philadelphia: Lea and Blanchard, 1845).

Fletcher, James Rupert, *The Biopolitics of Dementia: A Neurocritical Perspective* (London: Routledge, 2024).

Fletcher, James Rupert, 'Pathologisation, (Bio)medicalization and Biopolitics', in James Rupert Fletcher, James Rupert, and Andrea Capstick (eds.), *A Critical History of Dementia Studies* (London: Routledge, 2024), pp. 13–26.

Fletcher, James Rupert and Andrea Capstick, 'Introduction', in James Rupert Fletcher and Andrea Capstick (eds.), *A Critical History of Dementia Studies* (London: Routledge, 2024), pp. 1–9.

Fox, Patrick, 'From Senility to Alzheimer's Disease: The Rise of the Alzheimer's Disease Movement', *The Milbank Quarterly* 67:1 (1989): 58–102.

Frank, Arthur W., *The Wounded Storyteller: Body, Illness, and Ethics* (Chicago: University of Chicago Press, 1997).

Freud, Sigmund, *The Uncanny* (New York: Penguin, 2003).

Garland-Thomson, Rosemarie, *Extraordinary Bodies: Figuring Physical Disability in American Culture and Literature* (New York: Columbia University Press, 2017).

Garland-Thomson, Rosemarie, 'The Politics of Staring: Visual Rhetorics of Disability in Popular Photography', in Sharon L. Snyder, Brenda Jo Brueggemann, and Rosemarie Garland-Thomson (eds.), *Disability Studies: Enabling the Humanities* (New York: MLA, 2002), pp. 56–75.

Godwin, William, *Enquiry Concerning Political Justice, and its Influences on General Virtue and Happiness* (London: G.G.J. and J. Robinson, 1793).

Godwin, William, *St. Leon*, edited by William D. Brewer (Peterborough: Broadview Press, 2006).

Goldman, Marlene, *Forgotten: Narratives of Age-Related Dementia and Alzheimer's Disease in Canada* (Chicago: McGill-Queen's University Press, 2017).

Gullette, Margaret Morganroth, 'Against "Aging" – How to Talk about Growing Older', *Theory, Culture & Society* 35.7–8 (2018): 251–270.

Hartley, David, *Observations on Man: His Frame, His Duty, and His Expectations*, Vol. 1 (Cambridge: Cambridge University Press, 2013), pp. 268–415.

Heise-von der Lippe, Anya, 'Introduction: Post/human/Gothic', in Anya Heise-von der Lippe (ed.), *Posthuman Gothic* (Cardiff: University of Wales Press, 2017), pp. 1–16.

Hinton, Ladson, Yvette Fores, Carol Franz, Isabel Hernandez, and Linda S. Mitteness, 'The Borderlands of Primary Care Physician and Family Perspectives on "Troublesome" Behaviors of People with Dementia', in Annette Leibing and Lawrence Cohen (eds.), *Thinking about Dementia: Culture, Loss, and the Anthropology of Senility* (New Brunswick: Rutgers University Press, 2006), pp. 43–63.

Janowitz, Anne, 'The Romantic Fragment', in Duncan Wu (ed.), *A Companion to Romanticism* (Oxford: Blackwell, 2017), pp. 479–488.

Jenkins, Nick, 'Multi-Species Dementia Studies: How Moving Beyond Human Exceptionalism Can Advance Dementia's More Critical Turn', in Richard Ward and Linn J. Sandberg (eds.), *Critical Dementia Studies: An Introduction* (London: Routledge, 2023), pp. 72–82.

Jennings, Bruce, 'Cognition and Recognition in the Ethics of Dementia Care', in Marlene Goldman Kate de Medeiros and Thomas Cole (eds.), *Critical Humanities and Aging: Forging Interdisciplinary Dialogues* (London: Routledge, 2022), pp. 58–70.

Jewusiak, Jacob, *Aging, Duration, and the English Novel: Growing Old from Dickens to Woolf* (Cambridge: Cambridge University Press, 2019).

Juengst, Eric T., 'Anti-Aging Research and the Limits of Medicine', in Stephen G. Post and Robert H. Binstock (eds.), *The Fountain of Youth: Cultural, Scientific, and Ethical Perspectives on a Biomedical Goal* (Oxford: Oxford University Press, 2004), pp. 321–339.

Käll, Lisa Folkmarson and Kristin Zeiler, 'Still Alice?: Ethical Aspects of Conceptualising Selfhood in Dementia', in Alan Bleakley (ed.), *Routledge Handbook of the Medical Humanities* (London: Routledge, 2019), pp. 290–299.

Katz, Stephen and Annette Leibing, '"Lost in Time Like Tears in Rain": Critical Perspectives on Personhood and Dementia', in Richard Ward and Linn J. Sandberg (eds.), *Critical Dementia Studies: An Introduction* (London: Routledge, 2023), pp. 57–71.

Keetley, Dawn, 'The Shock of Aging (Women) in Horror Film', in Cynthia J. Miller and A. Bowdoin Van Riper (eds.), *Elder Horror: Essays on Film's Frightening Images of Aging* (Jefferson: McFarland, 2019), pp. 58–69.

Keller, Valerie, 'Children of Old Age? Infantilisation of People Living with Dementia', in Anna Wanka, Tabea Freutel-Funke, Sabine Andresen, and Frank Oswald et al. (eds.), *Linking Ages: A Dialogue between Childhood and Ageing Research* (London: Routledge, 2024), pp. 276–287.

Kelley, Sonaiya, 'Emily Mortimer Explains the "Extraordinary and Bizarre" Ending of "Relic"', *Los Angeles Times*, 10 July 2020, www.latimes.com/entertainment-arts/movies/story/2020-07-10/relic-ending-explained-emily-mortimer [last accessed 22 June 2025].

Kindell, Jackie, Aagje Swinnen, and John Keady, "Whose Story Is It and What Is It For?": Life Story as Critical Discourse in Dementia Studies', in James Rupert Fletcher and Andrea Capstick (eds.), *A Critical History of Dementia Studies* (London: Routledge, 2024), pp. 125–137.

King, Stephen, *Danse Macabre* (New York: Everest House, 1981).

Kitwood, Thomas, *Dementia Reconsidered, Revisited: The Person Still Comes First*, 2nd Ed., Dawn Brooker (ed.) (London: Open University Press, 2019).

Kotwasińska, Agnieszka, 'Un/re/production of Old Age in The Taking of Deborah Logan', *Somatechnics* 8.2 (2018): 178–194.

Kruger, Naomi, 'The "Terrifying Question Mark": Dementia, Fiction, and the Possibilities of Narrative', in Aagje Swinnen and Mark Schweda (eds.), *Popularizing Dementia: Public Expressions and Representations of Forgetfulness* (Bielefeld: Transcript, 2015), pp. 109–136.

Levinson, Marjorie, *The Romantic Fragment Poem: A Critique of a Form* (Chapel Hill: The University of North Carolina Press, 1986).

Ludwin, Katherine, '"On my good days, I can [...] almost pass for a normal person": Reading the Film Still Alice Using the Conceptual Lens of Heteronormativity', in James Rupert Fletcher and Andrea Capstick (eds.), *A Critical History of Dementia Studies* (London: Routledge, 2024), pp. 95–109.

Maginess, Tess, 'Introduction', in Tess Maginess (ed.), *Dementia and Literature: Interdisciplinary Perspectives* (London: Routledge, 2018), pp. 1–20.

The Manor, directed by Axelle Carolyn (Blumhouse Television, 2021).

Matthews, Nicole, 'Learning to Listen: Epistemic Injustice and Gothic Film in Dementia Care Education', *Feminist Media Studies* 16.6 (2016): 1078–1092.

Maturin, Charles, *Melmoth the Wanderer* (Oxford: Oxford World's Classics, 1989).

McGillvrey, Maddie, '"To Grandmother's House We Go": Documenting the Horror of the Aging Woman in Found Footage Films', in Cynthia J. Miller and A. Bowdoin Van Riper (eds.), *Elder Horror: Essays on Film's Frightening Images of Aging* (Jefferson: McFarland, 2019), pp. 70–80.

Miller, Cynthia J. and A. Bowdoin Van Riper, 'Introduction', in Cynthia J. Miller and A. Bowdoin Van Riper (eds.), *Elder Horror: Essays on Film's Frightening Images of Aging*, pp. 1–9.

Mills, Kirstin A., 'Haunted by "Lenore": The Fragment as Gothic Form, Creative Practice and Textual Evolution', *Gothic Studies* 23.2 (2021): 132–147.

Miquel-Baldellou, Marta, 'From the Female Grotesque to the Crone: Beware of the Older Woman in *The Taking of Deborah Logan* (2014)', in Noelia Gregorio-Fernández and Carmen M. Méndez-García (eds.), *Culture Wars and Horror Movies: Gender Debates in Post-2010's US Horror Cinema* (New York: Palgrave Macmillan, 2024), pp. 183–203.

Mitchell, David T. and Sharon L. Snyder, *Narrative Prosthesis: Disability and the Dependencies of Discourse* (Ann Arbor: University of Michigan Press, 2001).

NHS, 'What Is Dementia', *Health: A to Z*, 20 July 2023, www.nhs.uk/conditions/dementia/about-dementia/what-is-dementia/ [last accessed 16 November 2025].

NIH, 'Dementias', *Health Information*, 20 October 2025, www.ninds.nih.gov/health-information/disorders/dementias [last accessed 16 November 2025].

Old People, directed by Andy Fetscher (Constantin Television, 2022).

Oldfield, Margaret and Nancy Hansen, 'Power, Agency, Aging, and Cognitive Impairment', in Katie Aubrecht, Christine Kelly, and Carla Rice (eds.), *The Aging-Disability Nexus* (Toronto: UBC, 2020), pp. 130–144.

Ottaway, Susanna R., *The Decline of Life: Old Age in Eighteenth-Century England* (Cambridge: Cambridge University Press, 2004).

Oxford English Dictionary, 'dementia (n.)', March 2025, https://doi.org/10.1093/OED/7488111706.

Oyebode, Femi and Jan Oyebode, 'Personal Identity and Personhood: The Role of Fiction and Biographical Accounts in Dementia', in Tess Maginess (ed.), *Dementia and Literature: Interdisciplinary Perspectives* (London: Routledge, 2019), pp. 103–114.

Punter, David, *Gothic Pathologies: The Text, the Body and the Law* (New York: St. Martin's Press, 1998).

Quincy, John, *Lexicon Physico-Medicum; Or, a New Medicinal Dictionary Explaining the Difficult Terms Used in the Several Branches of the Profession and in Such Parts of Natural Philosophy*, 11th Ed. (London: Longman, 1794).

Rahilly, Joan, 'Language Breakdown and the Construction of Meaning: Linguistic Frameworks for Readings of Dementia in Literature', in Tess Maginess (ed.), *Dementia and Literature: Interdisciplinary Perspectives* (London: Routledge, 2019), pp. 115–132.

Relic, directed by Natalie Erika James (Nine Stories Productions, 2020).

The Rule of Jenny Pen, directed by James Ashcroft (Light in the Dark Productions, 2025).

Sacco, Donald F., Megan Walters, and Mitch Brown., 'Consumption of Psychological Horror is Associated with Reduced Stigmatization of Mental Illness', *Journal of Media Psychology: Theories, Methods, and Applications* 37. 3 (2024): 1–7.

Sandberg, Linn J. and Richard Ward, 'Introduction: Why Critical Dementia Studies and Why Now?' in Richard Ward and Linn J. Sandberg (eds.), *Critical Dementia Studies: An Introduction* (London: Routledge, 2023), pp. 1–12.

Sbaraini, Ella, 'The Ageing Body, Memory-Loss and Suicide in Georgian England', *Social History of Medicine* 35:1 (2021): 170–194.

Scrivner, Coltan, John A. Johnson, Jens Kjeldgaard-Christiansen, and Mathias Clasen, 'Pandemic Practice: Horror Fans and Morbidly Curious Individuals Are More Psychologically Resilient during the COVID-19 Pandemic', *Personality and Individual Differences*, 168 (2021), https://pmc.ncbi.nlm.nih.gov/articles/PMC7492010/.

Stillinger, Jack, 'The Multiple Versions of Coleridge's Poems: How Many "Mariners" Did Coleridge Write?' *Studies in Romanticism* 31:2 (Summer 1992): 127–146.

The Taking of Deborah Logan, directed by Adam Robitel (Guerin-Adler-Scott Pictures, 2014).

Thomas, Sophie, 'The Fragment', in Nicholas Roe (ed.), *Romanticism: An Oxford Guide* (Oxford: Oxford University Press, 2005), pp. 502–519.

Vermeulen, Pieter, 'Infrastructures of Aging: Form and Institutional Care in Dementia Fiction', *Poetics Today* 44:1–2 (June 2023): 15–35.

The Visit, directed by M. Night Shyamalan (Blumhouse, 2015).

Wasson, Sara, *Transplantation Gothic: Tissue Transfer in Literature, Film, and Medicine* (Manchester: Manchester University Press, 2020).

WHO, 'Dementia', *World Health Organization*, 31 March, 2025, www.who.int/news-room/fact-sheets/detail/dementia [last accessed 22 June 2025].

Willemsen, Steven and Miklós Kiss, 'Keeping Track of Time: The Role of Spatial and Embodied Cognition in the Comprehension of Nonlinear Storyworlds', *Style* 54:2 (2020): 172–198.

Wollstonecraft, Mary, *Maria; Or, the Wrongs of Woman*, edited by Anne K. Mellor (New York: W.W. Norton, 1994).

Wordsworth, William, 'The Prelude: Book XI', in Stephen Gill (ed.), *William Wordsworth: The Major Works* (Oxford: Oxford World's Classics, 2000), pp. 559–568.

Yoshizaki-Gibbons, Hailee M., 'Ageism and Ableism on the Silvering Screen: Entanglements of Disability and Ageing in Films Centred on Dementia', in Sarah Falcus, Heike Hartung, and Raquel Medina (eds.), *The Bloomsbury Handbook to Ageing in Contemporary Literature and Film* (London: Bloomsbury, 2023), pp. 281–292.

Zalloua, Zahi, 'Posthumanism', in Jeffrey R. Di Leo (ed.), *The Bloomsbury Handbook of Literary and Cultural Theory* (London: Bloomsbury, 2018), pp. 310–322.

Cambridge Elements

The Gothic

Dale Townshend
Manchester Metropolitan University
Dale Townshend is Professor of Gothic Literature in the Manchester Centre for Gothic Studies, Manchester Metropolitan University.

Angela Wright
University of Sheffield
Angela Wright is Professor of Romantic Literature in the School of English at the University of Sheffield and co-director of its Centre for the History of the Gothic.

Advisory Board
Enrique Ajuria Ibarra, *Universidad de las Américas, Puebla, Mexico*
Xavier Aldana Reyes, *Manchester Metropolitan University, UK*
Katarzyna Ancuta, *Chulalongkorn University, Thailand*
Carol Margaret Davison, *University of Windsor, Ontario, Canada*
Rebecca Duncan, *Linnaeus University, Sweden*
Jerrold E. Hogle, *Emeritus, University of Arizona*
Mark Jancovich, *University of East Anglia, UK*
Dawn Keetley, *Lehigh University, USA*
Roger Luckhurst, *Birkbeck College, University of London, UK*
Emma McEvoy, *University of Westminster, UK*
Eric Parisot, *Flinders University, Australia*
Andrew Smith, *University of Sheffield, UK*

About the Series
Seeking to publish short, research-led yet accessible studies of the foundational 'elements' within Gothic Studies as well as showcasing new and emergent lines of scholarly enquiry, this innovative series brings to a range of specialist and non-specialist readers some of the most exciting developments in recent Gothic scholarship.

Cambridge Elements

The Gothic

Elements in the Series

The Last Man and Gothic Sympathy
Michael Cameron

Democracy and the American Gothic
Michael J. Blouin

Dickens and the Gothic
Andrew Smith

Contemporary Body Horror
Xavier Aldana Reyes

The Music of the Gothic 1789–1820
Emma McEvoy

The Eternal Wanderer: The Eternal Wanderer
Mary Going

African American Gothic in the Era of Black Lives Matter
Maisha Wester

Biography and the Trade-Gothic Author: The Case of Isabella Kelly
Yael Shapira

Gothic Poland and British Fiction, c. 1790–1830
Jakub Lipski

Coastal Gothic, 1719–2020
Jimmy Packham

Disability and the Gothic: The Nineteenth Century
Essaka Joshua

Gothic Dementia: Troubled Minds in Gothic Timelines
Laura R. Kremmel

A full series listing is available at: www.cambridge.org/GOTH

For EU product safety concerns, contact us at Calle de José Abascal, 56–1°, 28003 Madrid, Spain or eugpsr@cambridge.org.

www.ingramcontent.com/pod-product-compliance
Lightning Source LLC
LaVergne TN
LVHW011854060526
838200LV00054B/4334